Third Grade Skills

A Best Value Book™

Written by
Patricia Pedigo and Dr. Roger DeSanti

Edited by
Kelley and Aaron Levy

Obtuse - Fat
Acute - Smaller
Rt Angle - Corners

© Carson-Dellosa CD-3760

ISBN 0-88724-545-5

Table of Contents

Third Grade Skills

Written by Patricia Pedigo and Dr. Roger DeSanti
Edited by Kelley and Aaron Levy

About the Authors

Patricia Pedigo has many years of teaching experience in urban, rural, public, and private settings. She has taught at all elementary and middle school grade levels, and worked as a reading specialist for learning different students. Patricia has created materials that integrate content areas with language development skills. She holds a M.Ed. in Reading Education and is nearing completion of her doctoral studies.

Dr. Roger DeSanti has been an educator since the mid-1970s. His teaching experiences span a wide range of grades and ability levels, from deaf nurseries through university graduate schools. As a professor, he has authored numerous articles and books, achievement tests, and instructional materials.

Perfect for school or home, every **Kelley Wingate Best Value Book™** has been designed to help students master the skills necessary to succeed. Each book is packed with reproducible test pages, 96 cut-apart flash cards, and supplemental resource pages full of valuable information, ideas, and activities. These activities may be used as classroom or homework activities, or as enrichment material.

This book was developed to provide skills practice in the areas of Reading, Grammar, and Mathematics. Each skill is identified and presented in a range of grade-appropriate ability levels. These activities have been sequenced to facilitate successful completion of the assigned tasks, thus building the self-confidence students need to meet academic challenges.

Ready-to-Use Ideas and Activities

Included in the back of this book are 48 vocabulary and 48 math flash cards ideal for individual review, group solving sessions, or as part of timed, sequential, or grouped activities. Pull out the flash card pages and cut the cards apart with scissors or a paper cutter. Here are just a few of the ways you may want to use these flash cards:

Vocabulary Flash Cards

Bingo Reproduce the Bingo sheet (page iii) for every student. Write the vocabulary flash card words on a chart or chalkboard. Have students choose 24 words and write one in each block of their bingo cards. Cut out the vocabulary flash cards and make them into a deck. Rather than calling out the word itself, call out a definition, antonym, or synonym for the word. Place the called-out words in a separate stack. Students who have the word being described written on their bingo cards should make an "X" through the word. The first student who crosses out five words in a row (horizontally, vertically, or diagonally) wins the game. Check his bingo card against the stack of called-out words. To extend the game, continue playing until students have crossed out all the words on their Bingo cards.

Clue A group of 4 students (teams of 2) can use the vocabulary cards to play "clue." Have children place the cards face down in the middle of a table. The first player selects a card and then gives a one-word clue that describes that word to his partner. If his partner cannot guess the word being suggested, the selected card is given to a member of the opposing team who attempts to get his partner to guess the word. Teams take turns guessing until someone can name the word on the card. The first team to name the word wins a point.

Writing Students can choose cards at random and write a sentence with each word, or write paragraphs or short stories using several of the flash card words.

Vocabulary Write sentences on the board using the vocabulary words but leave blanks in place of the vocabulary words. Have small groups of students take turns sorting through the flash cards to find words that could complete the sentences accurately.

Math Flash Cards

Timed Exercises Use a timer or stopwatch to record how many problems a student can answer correctly in a certain amount of time. Review incorrect answers and repeat the exercise. Provide rewards for improved scores.

Quizzes Use flash cards as impromptu quizzes. Give each student three to five cards attached to an answer sheet that he can complete and return. Vary the selection of cards given to each student for each quiz.

Bonus Questions Post a certain number of cards as bonus questions or for extra credit.

B	I	N	G	O
		FREE		

Name _____   Skill: Blends

Rule
If two or more consonants appear next to each other in a word and you hear the sound of each letter, the sound is called a **blend**.
*bl*anket   *tr*ain   *st*op

Complete the word under each picture by writing the missing blend.

f l ower   s l ide   g l ue

t r ee   d r um   p l ate

b r oom   s n ake   f r uit

s w ing   s k ate   s t ar

1

Name _____

Rule

If two or more consonants appear next to each other in a word and you hear the sound of each letter, the sound is called a **blend**.

*bl*anket   *tr*ain   ***st***op

Complete the word under each picture by writing the missing blend.

p l an   b l anket   c r ayon

d r ess   g r apes   s t ove

s k irt   p l anet   c r own

fore s t   f r og   de s k

© Carson-Dellosa CD-3760   2

Name _____   Skill: Blends

Rule
If two or more consonants appear next to each other in a word and you hear the sound of each letter, the sound is called a **blend**.

*bl*anket   *tr*ain   *st*op

Complete the word under each picture by writing the missing blend.

b l o c k   s n o w   f l o w e r

c l o c k   s t o o l   p r e s e n t

p r i z e   t r a i n   b r e a d

b r i c k s   f l a g   d r i v e

3

Rule

If two or more consonants appear next to each other in a word and you hear the sound of each letter, the sound is called a **blend**.

*bl*anket   *tr*ain   *st*op

Complete the word under each picture by writing the missing blend.

p r ice   s t ore   s l eep

s t orm   p l ane   c l ay

c l own   b r ain   m a s k

s n ail   ba s k et   p l ant

Rule

Short vowel sounds are:

      a as in **pat**   **e** as in **pet**   **i** as in **pit**   **o** as in **pot**   **u** as in **put**

Read each word. Decide which sound the underlined vowel makes. Put the words with the short vowel sounds into the correct groups below. Not all the words will be used.

paint	neck	pile
pan	neat	pint
dance	jelly	rise
fancy	gentle	pickle
ham	eagle	spin
gasp	den	smile
maid	belly	sip
maple	deep	ribbon
jail	beam	rim
jacket	mend	lid
hand	smell	nip

Sounds like the "a" **in *pat***	**Sounds like the "e"** **in *pet***	**Sounds like the "i"** **in *pit***

_____   _____   _____

_____   _____   _____

_____   _____   _____

_____   _____   _____

_____   _____   _____

_____   _____   _____

Think of a new word for each group (**short a**, **e**, and **i**).

_____   _____   _____

Rule

Short vowel sounds are:

    a as in **pat**   **e** as in **pet**   **i** as in **pit**   **o** as in **pot**   **u** as in **put**

Read each word. Decide which sound the underlined vowel makes. Put the words with the short vowel sounds into the correct groups below. Not all the words will be used.

d<u>i</u>ve	b<u>o</u>ttle	p<u>u</u>ppy
b<u>i</u>t	bl<u>o</u>ck	b<u>u</u>g
br<u>i</u>ng	dr<u>o</u>p	<u>u</u>se
br<u>i</u>dge	br<u>o</u>ke	j<u>u</u>nk
<u>i</u>ce	als<u>o</u>	tr<u>u</u>th
p<u>ie</u>	l<u>o</u>g	b<u>u</u>mp
d<u>i</u>g	l<u>o</u>ck	c<u>u</u>p
h<u>i</u>ss	p<u>o</u>em	f<u>u</u>zz
th<u>i</u>n	tr<u>o</u>t	t<u>u</u>be
wh<u>i</u>sper	h<u>o</u>g	d<u>u</u>st
s<u>i</u>ght	<u>oi</u>l	s<u>u</u>per

Sounds like the "i" in *pit*	**Sounds like the "o" in *pot***	**Sounds like the "u" in *put***

_____ _____ _____

_____ _____ _____

_____ _____ _____

_____ _____ _____

_____ _____ _____

Think of a new word for each group (**short i**, **o**, and **u**).

_____ _____ _____

Rule
Short vowel sounds are:
a as in **pat**   **e** as in **pet**   **i** as in **pit**   **o** as in **pot**   **u** as in **put**

Read each word. Decide which sound the underlined vowel makes. Put the words with the short vowel sounds into the correct groups below. Not all the words will be used.

t<u>i</u>me	b<u>o</u>ther	<u>u</u>nit
cl<u>i</u>p	ch<u>o</u>p	t<u>u</u>g
sk<u>i</u>n	c<u>o</u>mmon	f<u>u</u>ture
d<u>i</u>m	<u>o</u>we	t<u>u</u>nnel
sl<u>i</u>de	r<u>o</u>cket	<u>u</u>gly
r<u>i</u>pe	sp<u>oi</u>l	sw<u>u</u>ng
d<u>i</u>nner	f<u>o</u>nd	tr<u>ue</u>
f<u>i</u>ddle	w<u>o</u>ve	<u>u</u>nder
m<u>i</u>st	j<u>o</u>lly	s<u>u</u>dden
t<u>i</u>p	c<u>o</u>de	j<u>u</u>st
p<u>i</u>ne	m<u>o</u>p	r<u>u</u>le

Sounds like the "i" in *pit*	**Sounds like the "o" in *pot***	**Sounds like the "u" in *put***

_____	_____	_____
_____	_____	_____
_____	_____	_____
_____	_____	_____
_____	_____	_____
_____	_____	_____

Think of a new word for each group (**short i**, **o**, and **u**).

_____   _____   _____

Rule
Short vowel sounds are:
a as in **pat**   **e** as in **pet**   **i** as in **pit**   **o** as in **pot**   **u** as in **put**

Read each word. Decide which sound the underlined vowel makes. Put the words with the short vowel sounds into the correct groups below. Not all the words will be used.

<u>a</u>nimal	<u>e</u>ven	m<u>u</u>ch
beg<u>a</u>n	w<u>e</u>nt	p<u>u</u>pil
<u>a</u>te	sp<u>e</u>ll	j<u>u</u>st
m<u>a</u>de	n<u>e</u>xt	c<u>u</u>t
st<u>a</u>nd	m<u>e</u>	Jan<u>u</u>ary
h<u>a</u>ppen	z<u>e</u>bra	f<u>u</u>nny
t<u>a</u>ble	<u>e</u>mpty	n<u>u</u>mber
sh<u>a</u>pe	wh<u>e</u>n	h<u>u</u>man
<u>a</u>nswer	<u>e</u>gg	h<u>u</u>ndred
b<u>a</u>ck	<u>e</u>njoy	fr<u>u</u>it
pl<u>a</u>nt	s<u>e</u>cret	s<u>u</u>mmer
Sounds like the "a" in *pat*	**Sounds like the "e" in *pet***	**Sounds like the "u" in *put***

_____   _____   _____

_____   _____   _____

_____   _____   _____

_____   _____   _____

_____   _____   _____

_____   _____   _____

Think of a new word for each group (**short a**, **e**, and **u**).

_____   _____   _____

Rule
Long vowels say their names: **a** as in **lace**   **e** as in **easy**   **i** as in **ice**   **o** as in **open**   **u** as in **tuba**

Read the words in each box. Decide which sound the underlined vowel makes. Put the words with the long vowel sound into the correct group below. Not all the words will be used.

m<u>a</u>le	b<u>e</u>an	l<u>i</u>st
<u>a</u>nswer	l<u>e</u>af	f<u>i</u>lm
l<u>a</u>zy	str<u>ee</u>t	p<u>i</u>pe
c<u>a</u>r	<u>o</u>ver	b<u>i</u>te
tom<u>a</u>to	<u>e</u>qual	<u>i</u>dle
b<u>a</u>by	w<u>e</u>	w<u>i</u>re
f<u>a</u>ll	childr<u>e</u>n	sp<u>i</u>der
sh<u>a</u>pe	<u>ea</u>gle	w<u>i</u>de
beg<u>a</u>n	thr<u>ee</u>	l<u>i</u>fe
pl<u>a</u>y	<u>e</u>nd	gr<u>i</u>p
b<u>a</u>ke	l<u>e</u>ft	<u>i</u>ll

Sounds like the "a" in *lace*	**Sounds like the "e" in *easy***	**Sounds like the "i" in *ice***

_____   _____   _____

_____   _____   _____

_____   _____   _____

_____   _____   _____

_____   _____   _____

_____   _____   _____

Think of a new word for each group (**long a**, **e**, and **i**).

_____   _____   _____

Rule

Long vowels say their names:

    a as in **lace**   **e** as in **easy**   **i** as in **ice**   **o** as in **open**   **u** as in **tuba**

Read the words in each box. Decide which sound the underlined vowel makes. Put the words with the long vowel sound into the correct group below. Not all the words will be used.

quite	over	fur
fire	joy	tube
wife	hero	ruin
nine	stop	push
with	joke	sugar
insect	bowl	tuna
until	toll	tune
iron	pole	flute
spine	job	June
price	go	unit
which	cow	bull

Sounds like the "i" in *ice*	**Sounds like the "o" in *open***	**Sounds like the "u" in *tuba***
_____	_____	_____
_____	_____	_____
_____	_____	_____
_____	_____	_____
_____	_____	_____
_____	_____	_____

Think of a new word for each group (**long i**, **o**, and **u**).

_____   _____   _____

Rule
Long vowels say their names: **a** as in **lace**   **e** as in **easy**   **i** as in **ice**   **o** as in **open**   **u** as in **tuba**

Read the words in each box. Decide which sound the underlined vowel makes. Put the words with the long vowel sound into the correct group below. Not all the words will be used.

begin	bone	mule
with	drop	duty
ripe	ocean	up
white	stone	February
light	bottom	crude
mint	awoke	unless
still	float	hunt
knife	body	July
wild	odd	sudden
hike	owner	useful
fine	know	tulip

Sounds like the "i" in *ice*	Sounds like the "o" in *open*	Sounds like the "u" in *tuba*

_____   _____   _____

_____   _____   _____

_____   _____   _____

_____   _____   _____

_____   _____   _____

_____   _____   _____

Think of a new word for each group (**long i**, **o**, and **u**).

_____   _____   _____

Rule

Long vowels say their names:

  a as in **lace**   **e** as in **easy**   **i** as in **ice**   **o** as in **open**   **u** as in **tuba**

Read the words in each box. Decide which sound the underlined vowel makes. Put the words with the long vowel sound into the correct group below. Not all the words will be used.

had	really	rude
black	evil	regular
fast	feather	untie
wait	cheese	much
mail	clean	include
chain	ready	unite
radio	pea	truth
able	ten	suit
ape	teeth	jump
today	peach	upset
that	tell	music

| **Sounds like the "a" in *lace*** | **Sounds like the "e" in *easy*** | **Sounds like the "u" in *tuba*** |

_____   _____   _____

_____   _____   _____

_____   _____   _____

_____   _____   _____

_____   _____   _____

_____   _____   _____

Think of a new word for each group (**long a, e,** and **u**).

_____   _____   _____

Rule

Different words that have almost the same meaning are called **synonyms**.
Beautiful and *lovely* are synonyms.

Read the sentences and choices below. Circle the word that is a synonym for the word that is underlined in the sentence.

1. Joseph will <u>glue</u> the model plane together.
   tie   (paste)   staple

2. I was <u>anxious</u> about flying for the first time.
   (worried)   mad   sick

3. The cupboard is <u>above</u> the sink.
   in   under   (over)

4. Rosie was <u>afraid</u> of the monster in the movie.
   brave   (scared)   happy

5. Harry is in the third grade. Mike is <u>also</u> in the third grade.
   (too)   almost   not

6. John will <u>dash</u> to the store to buy the milk for his mother.
   fly   walk   (run)

7. Perry <u>invited</u> seventeen boys to his birthday party.
   (asked)   brought   fed

8. This is the <u>final</u> test you will take this week.
   first   only   (last)

9. Katie needed to <u>repair</u> the broken skate.
   (fix)   break   sell

10. That <u>lady</u> is my favorite aunt.
   man   (woman)   girl

Rule

Different words that have almost the same meaning are called **synonyms**.
Beautiful and *lovely* are synonyms.

Read the sentences and choices below. Circle the word that is a synonym for the word that is underlined in the sentence.

1. Martha is standing <u>behind</u> Peggy in line.

   next   **before**   **after**

2. The <u>small</u> bird fell from its nest in the tree.

   big   **scared**   **little**

3. Kendal had a very <u>clever</u> idea that we all liked.

   funny   **smart**   **silly**

4. Bury the seeds under one inch of <u>soil</u>.

   dirt   **water**   **paper**

5. Hans kicked the ball <u>beyond</u> the back fence.

   into   **over**   **further**

6. When the baby is hungry, he becomes <u>loud</u>.

   angry   **noisy**   **older**

7. Wear your sunglasses because it is <u>bright</u> today.

   sunny   **cloudy**   **hot**

8. I will walk to the library because it is <u>nearby</u>.

   quick   **important**   **close**

9. Pam wore a sweater because it was <u>chilly</u> in the theater.

   hot   **cool**   **frozen**

10. We will go to the restaurant to <u>dine</u> this evening.

    cook   **talk**   **eat**

Name _____   Skill: Synonyms

<table>
<tr><td colspan="1">Rule</td></tr>
</table>

Rule
Different words that have almost the same meaning are called **synonyms**.
Beautiful and *lovely* are synonyms.

Read the sentences and choices below. Circle the word that is a synonym for the word that is underlined in the sentence.

1. Jeremy had an <u>awful</u> cold last winter.
   good   **terrible**   **gentle**

2. Be careful not to <u>tear</u> your paper!
   wrinkle   **tape**   **rip**

3. The boat began to <u>sink</u> when it hit the rock.
   fall   **tip**   **float**

4. The puppy was <u>unhappy</u> when we left the pet store.
   sad   **scared**   **glad**

5. The deer <u>sniffed</u> the air when it heard a strange noise.
   smelled   **tossed**   **stopped**

6. It was <u>difficult</u> to say good-bye to my best friend.
   fun   **easy**   **hard**

7. The umbrella was still a little <u>damp</u> from the rain this morning.
   loose   **wet**   **dry**

8. My family went to a <u>banquet</u> in the old castle and we ate too much.
   ghost   **feast**   **dance**

9. Roger is the <u>author</u> of that story.
   reader   **listen**   **writer**

10. It was time to pack our bags and say <u>farewell</u> to our cousins.
    good-bye   **hello**   **exclaim**

Rule

Words that have opposite meanings are called **antonyms**.

Before and *after* are antonyms.

Read the sentences and choices below. Circle the word that means the opposite as the word that is underlined in the sentence.

1. That <u>lady</u> has the keys to the car.

    gentleman   **woman**   **aunt**

2. Those shoes are <u>mine</u>.

    his   **yours**   **ours**

3. Jenny has a <u>bunch</u> of pencils in her desk.

    many   **lot**   **few**

4. Please help me lift this <u>heavy</u> box.

    small   **light**   **big**

5. Our class just <u>finished</u> reading chapter two.

    ended   **began**   **enjoyed**

6. Kaitlyn thinks her drawing is <u>ugly</u>.

    pretty   **simple**   **bad**

7. Cassie <u>won</u> the spelling bee for our school.

    entered   **played**   **lost**

8. Did you see that <u>tiny</u> mark on Dad's new car?

    small   **large**   **dent**

9. It is time to <u>raise</u> the flag.

    salute   **fold**   **lower**

10. Justin is the <u>quickest</u> runner in the group.

    slowest   **fastest**   **smartest**

16

Rule

Words that have opposite meanings are called **antonyms**.

Before and *after* are antonyms.

Read the sentences and choices below. Circle the word that means the opposite as the word that is underlined in the sentence.

1. The show is just <u>beginning</u>!

   starting   **wonderful**   **ending**

2. Please <u>close</u> the window.

   open   **clean**   **shut**

3. Are you still <u>asleep</u>?

   sleeping   **awake**   **reading**

4. Put on an <u>old</u> shirt for this job.

   dirty   **white**   **new**

5. The pitcher threw the ball and the batter <u>missed</u> it.

   hit   **threw**   **caught**

6. You are acting like an <u>adult</u>.

   baby   **clown**   **boy**

7. The child was <u>smiling</u> at the puppy.

   shaking   **grinning**   **frowning**

8. Did you make sure that the door was <u>locked</u>?

   solid   **unlocked**   **closed**

9. Why is Meghan so <u>cheerful</u> today?

   happy   **gloomy**   **helpful**

10. The sky is so <u>clear</u> today!

    pretty   **blue**   **cloudy**

Rule

Words that have opposite meanings are called **antonyms**.

Before and *after* are antonyms.

Read the sentences and choices below. Circle the word that means the opposite as the word that is underlined in the sentence.

1. It is <u>easy</u> for Jay to lift that heavy box.

   difficult   **strong**   **silly**

2. Adam arrived <u>early</u> for the party.

   late   **after**   **before**

3. I <u>never</u> like to eat pizza.

   rarely   **seldom**   **always**

4. You gave me the <u>wrong</u> answer to that question.

   other   **right**   **simple**

5. Did you <u>receive</u> a letter written for Milly?

   write   **send**   **get**

6. Autumn is my <u>favorite</u> season.

   loved   **disliked**   **warm**

7. Do not <u>drag</u> your book bag down the hall!

   pull   **push**   **carry**

8. Susan was really <u>calm</u> during the storm.

   excited   **quiet**   **still**

9. The girls were <u>noisy</u> as they entered the school.

   quiet   **running**   **loud**

10. Giving you a ride was the <u>least</u> I could do.

   only   **nice**   **most**

Rule

Words that are pronounced the same way but have different meanings and spellings are called **homophones**.

Flower and *flour* are homophones.

Read the sentences and choices below. For each sentence, write the correct homophone in the blank.

1. An _____ crawled across the sidewalk.

   ant   **aunt**

2. There are _____ colors in my rainbow.

   ate   **eight**

3. _____ am nine years old.

   I   **eye**

4. Can you _____ big numbers?

   ad   **add**

5. That _____ is building a hive.

   be   **bee**

6. Where did the dog _____ his bone?

   berry   **bury**

7. The wind _____ hard last night!

   blew   **blue**

8. I used the _____ to stop my bike.

   brakes   **breaks**

9. How much ice cream did you _____ ?

   buy   **by**   **bye**

10. Rachel _____ a letter to her friend.

   cent   **scent**   **sent**

Name _____   Skill: Homophones

> **Rule**
>
> Words that are pronounced the same way but have different meanings and spellings are called **homophones**.
>
> *Flower* and *flour* are homophones.

Read the sentences and choices below. For each sentence, write the correct homophone in the blank.

1. That _____ is flying awfully low!

   plain   **plane**

2. What game did you _____ to play?

   choose   **chews**

3. Pick up those _____ and hang them up!

   close   **clothes**

4. Winston sailed his toy boat down the _____ .

   creak   **creek**

5. Mom _____ my shirt blue.

   died   **dyed**

6. That rabbit's _____ makes me sneeze!

   fir   **fur**

7. A bluebird _____ to the maple tree.

   flew   **flu**

8. Use two cups of _____ to make this cake.

   flour   **flower**

9. Kyle _____ everything on the test.

   new   **knew**   **gnu**

10. Would you like milk _____ soda to drink?

    oar   **or**   **ore**

Name _____   Skill: Homophones

Rule

Words that are pronounced the same way but have different meanings and spellings are called **homophones**.

Flower and *flour* are homophones.

Read the sentences and choices below. For each sentence, write the correct homophone in the blank.

1. Sylvia has _____ two inches this year!

             groan   **grown**

2. Janie _____ the wrong answer.

            guessed   **guest**

3. Neville put the blocks into three _____ .

             rows   **rose**

4. I could not _____ what you just said.

            hear   **here**

5. The fence was too _____ to climb over.

            hi   **high**

6. Rodney ate the _____ pie by himself!

            hole   **whole**

7. _____ house is not very large.

            Hour   **Our**

8. The stars come out at _____ .

            knight   **night**

9. The Smith family lost _____ dog.

            they're   **their**   **there**

10. Are you going _____ the circus with us?

            to   **two**   **too**

Rule
Words that we understand and use in our daily language are called our **vocabulary**.

Complete each sentence by circling the correct word.

1. A word that means <u>to trip or lose your footing</u> is ...
   squeeze   **purpose**   **stumble**

2. To <u>keep safe</u> is to ...
   snatch   **supply**   **protect**

3. A <u>place to eat food</u> is a ...
   pronounce   **restaurant**   **thrust**

4. The word <u>mend</u> means ...
   interrupt   **musical**   **fix**

5. Another word for <u>street</u> is ...
   approach   **avenue**   **continue**

6. To <u>be well known</u> is to be ...
   famous   **fearful**   **funny**

7. When you <u>want to know more about something</u> you are ...
   cactus   **correct**   **curious**

8. Another word for <u>test</u> is ...
   exam   **embarrass**   **award**

9. A word that means <u>to take air in and out of your lungs</u> is ...
   breathe   **bathe**   **detail**

10. A person who is <u>unable to see</u> is ...
    thirsty   **blind**   **cute**

Rule
Words that we understand and use in our daily language are called our **vocabulary**.

Complete each sentence by circling the correct word.

1. A word that means <u>the day before today</u> is ...
   yesterday   **tomorrow**   **behold**

2. To <u>disappear</u> is to ...
   watch   **vanish**   **trumpet**

3. A <u>group of twelve</u> is a ...
   dozen   **tortoise**   **trickle**

4. A word that means <u>to get ready</u> is ...
   prevent   **stew**   **prepare**

5. Another word for <u>rare</u> is ...
   position   **unusual**   **startle**

6. To <u>make something pointed</u> is to ...
   sharpen   **silence**   **rattle**

7. When you <u>talk something over with another person</u> you ...
   discuss   **dusk**   **bounce**

8. Another word for <u>real</u> is ...
   admire   **actual**   **account**

9. A <u>short coat</u> is a ...
   guitar   **helmet**   **jacket**

10. A person who <u>flies a plane</u> is a ...
   borrow   **dentist**   **pilot**

Name _____ Skill: Vocabulary

Rule

Words that we understand and use in our daily language are called our **vocabulary**.

Complete each sentence by circling the correct word.

1. A word that means <u>far away</u> is ...
   carve   **dare**   **distant**

2. To <u>address with kind wishes</u> is to ...
   fig   **grind**   **greet**

3. A <u>grown-up person</u> is an ...
   adult   **alphabet**   **audience**

4. Another word for <u>trap</u> is ...
   cliff   **capture**   **fellow**

5. The word <u>eager</u> means ...
   carriage   **disturb**   **anxious**

6. To <u>decide on something</u> is to ...
   choose   **calm**   **bandage**

7. When you <u>make something new</u> you ...
   create   **double**   **bore**

8. Another word for <u>afraid</u> is ...
   familiar   **farewell**   **fearful**

9. A word that means <u>total or all</u> is ...
   dawn   **entire**   **faint**

10. <u>A person who cuts meat</u> is a ...
   designer   **butcher**   **carpenter**

Rule
Words that have something in common can be sorted into groups called **categories**. pencil (school supply)　　　　tent (camping supply) paper (school supply)　　　　sleeping bag (camping supply)

All of these words belong to the same big category. Name how they are alike in the "Main Heading." Sort the words into two groups, or subcategories. Put the title of each group on the line "Subheading."

orange	**onion**	**raspberry**	**spinach**
carrot	**apple**	**radish**	**cherry**
celery	**beet**	**lettuce**	**grape**
plum	**banana**	**lemon**	**squash**
blueberry	**potato**	**peach**	**peas**

Main Heading:	
Subheading:	**Subheading:**

Rule

Words that have something in common can be sorted into groups called **categories**.

pencil (school supply)   tent (camping supply)

paper (school supply)   sleeping bag (camping supply)

All of these words belong to the same big category. Name how they are alike in the "Main Heading." Sort the words into two groups, or subcategories. Put the title of each group on the line "Subheading."

Ellen	Mark	Nancy	Jane
George	Joe	Paul	Bob
Cindy	Mary	Anne	Marsha
David	Peter	Greg	Mike
Diana	Larry	Peggy	Laura

Main Heading:	
Subheading:	**Subheading:**

Name _____

Rule
Words that have something in common can be sorted into groups called **categories**. pencil (school supply)　　　　tent (camping supply) paper (school supply)　　　　sleeping bag (camping supply)

All of these words belong to the same big category. Name how they are alike in the "Main Heading." Sort the words into two groups, or subcategories. Put the title of each group on the line "Subheading."

store	King Library	Yellowstone Park	hospital
park	D.C. High School	bridge	Las Vegas
Elm Avenue	Main Street Mall	building	river
school	street	Golden Gate Bridge	library
city	Care Hospital	Mississippi River	Super Dome

Main Heading:

Subheading:	Subheading:

Rule

When you come to a word you don't know, use the **context clues** (the meaning of the rest of the sentence or paragraph) to help you understand its meaning.

Use the context clues to figure out the meaning of each underlined word below. Circle the correct meaning.

1. The oil made the street <u>slick</u>, and the car tires slid on it.

   slippery   **sticky**   **sweet**

2. Brian was filled with <u>grief</u> when his best friend moved away.

   happiness   **hate**   **sadness**

3. Kelsey put the money into a <u>pouch</u> she kept on her belt.

   bag   **dress**   **bottle**

4. We don't have much time, so please give a <u>brief</u> speech.

   nasty   **slow**   **short**

5. I <u>plunged</u> right into the pool, but my sister took her time getting wet.

   waded   **jumped**   **pulled**

6. We will <u>release</u> the bird from the cage when its broken wing is better.

   hide   **capture**   **set free**

7. We baked a <u>batch</u> of cookies for the bake sale.

   one   **group**   **kind**

8. This <u>antique</u> chair was used by a king.

   pretty   **very old**   **new**

9. The directions tell us to <u>combine</u> the eggs and flour to make the cake.

   separate   **sell**   **mix**

10. Use <u>caution</u> when trying to cross a busy street.

   safety   **rudeness**   **cars**

<table>
<tr><td>Rule
When you come to a word you don't know, use the context clues (the meaning of the rest of the sentence or paragraph) to help you understand its meaning.</td></tr>
</table>

Use the context clues to figure out the meaning of each underlined word below. Circle the correct meaning.

1. My face turned <u>crimson</u> when I blushed.

    green   **red**   **pale**

2. The <u>gravel</u> in the driveway crunched under the tires of the car.

    grass   **small stones**   **cement**

3. I did not <u>hesitate</u> to help when the old man fell down the steps.

    wait   **jump**   **move**

4. We put the books in a <u>crate</u> before we shipped them to Mexico.

    wastebasket   **wooden box**   **bag**

5. I <u>detest</u> that television show!

    enjoy   **love**   **dislike**

6. The umbrella wouldn't open, so it was <u>useless</u>.

    not helpful   **nice**   **broken**

7. The beef was <u>tough</u> to chew.

    soft   **tasty**   **hard**

8. The room began to <u>sway</u> when the earthquake hit.

    rock   **light up**   **sing**

9. Don't just tear the paper. <u>Shred</u> it so no one can read it.

    make tiny pieces   **tape together**   **throw away**

10. Shelly was so <u>timid</u>, she hid when the children came over to play.

    old   **shy**   **pretty**

Rule
When you come to a word you don't know, use the **context clues** (the meaning of the rest of the sentence or paragraph) to help you understand its meaning.

Use the context clues to figure out the meaning of each underlined word below. Circle the correct meaning.

1. My legs <u>tremble</u> when I am scared.

   shake　　　　　　　**faint**　　　　　　　**strong**

2. The bakery had <u>various</u> types of cookies from which we could choose.

   one　　　　　　　**different**　　　　　　　**none**

3. The chocolate milk shake was a <u>tasty</u> treat!

   good　　　　　　　**awful**　　　　　　　**ugly**

4. We squinted our eyes as we walked outside into the <u>brilliant</u> light.

   dull　　　　　　　**bright**　　　　　　　**new**

5. Trevor began to <u>argue</u> with his sister over who would get the new game.

   tease　　　　　　　**talk**　　　　　　　**fight**

6. Trenice walked down the <u>aisle</u> of the theater, looking for a good seat.

   pathway　　　　　　　**screen**　　　　　　　**building**

7. The fuzzy peach <u>flesh</u> felt soft as a baby mouse!

   feet　　　　　　　**skin**　　　　　　　**cage**

8. Ten dollars seems <u>expensive</u> for a kite.

   costly　　　　　　　**cheap**　　　　　　　**soft**

9. Larry <u>deserves</u> a reward for that brave deed.

   earns　　　　　　　**gives**　　　　　　　**decides**

10. I cannot <u>recall</u> how many children were at the party last week.

    tell　　　　　　　**speak**　　　　　　　**remember**

Name _____   Skill: Context Clues

> **Rule**
> When you come to a word you don't know, use the **context clues** (the meaning of the rest of the sentence or paragraph) to help you understand its meaning.

Use the context clues to figure out the meaning of each underlined word below. Circle the correct meaning.

1. This <u>route</u> to the grocery store takes me past your house.
   travel   **way**   **cart**

2. We saw clowns and rode the roller coaster at the <u>carnival</u>.
   camp   **parade**   **fair**

3. Mr. Spade will <u>conduct</u> the orchestra next week.
   feed   **lead**   **move**

4. The young boy began to <u>wail</u> when he could not find his mother.
   jump   **cry**   **bang**

5. I <u>intend</u> to find out who took my watch!
   plan   **hate**   **will not**

6. We must <u>divide</u> this box of apples into two groups.
   separate   **crust**   **lift**

7. Jonas felt <u>cozy</u> under the warm blankets.
   cold   **frightened**   **snug**

8. The fresh paint looked <u>glossy</u> in the sun.
   shiny   **dull**   **blue**

9. The hoot of the owl sounded <u>eerie</u> in the darkness.
   stubborn   **strange**   **happy**

10. The glass vase <u>shattered</u> when it hit the floor.
    dented   **broke**   **rang out**

Rule

Understanding what happens in a story is called **comprehension.**

Read the story, then answer the questions about it.

    Greg and Calvin hopped off the subway at the stadium. Today was the biggest game of the baseball season, but neither boy had a ticket. They seemed to be in luck. No one was standing in line for tickets! As they reached the ticket booth, they saw why. A large sign said, "SOLD OUT!" Greg and Calvin could hear the crowd roar as the game began. They were very disappointed. The boys began to walk across the parking lot, back to the subway. The crowd behind them roared again as a ball flew over the wall and landed near their feet. Maybe this game would be fun after all!

1. **A good title for this story would be:**
   a. A Ride on the Subway
   b. Baseball in the Parking Lot
   c. The Roar of the Crowd
2. **What were the boys hoping to buy?**_____

   _____

3. **What is a word that means "a sports park or arena"?**
   a. roared
   b. disappointed
   c. stadium
4. **Why couldn't the boys get in to see the game?**_____

   _____

5. **What happened that made the boys happy about the game?**_____

   _____

6. **What would you do if you were the boys?**_____

   _____

> **Rule**
> Understanding what happens in a story is called **comprehension.**

Read the story, then answer the questions about it.

Nan blushed as the teacher called her name. It was her turn to stand in front of the class and give her book report. Nan slowly pulled out her paper and stood up. Her feet felt heavy as she walked to the front of the room. She could feel the eyes of every person in the class watching her, waiting for her to begin. Nan did not even look at the class as she began to read. The first word out of her mouth sounded just like a frog croaking! Nan turned red and cleared her throat. She wished she could just disappear. Writing reports was fun, but giving them was difficult.

1. **A good title for this story would be:**
   a. The Book Report
   b. The Class Laughs
   c. The Frogs are Croaking
2. **Why does Nan walk to the front of the room?**_____

   _____
3. **What is a word that means "turned red"?**
   a. disappear
   b. heavy
   c. blushed
4. **How does Nan feel about giving reports to the class?**_____

   _____
5. **Name two things in the story that show us how Nan is feeling.**_____

   _____
6. **What could Nan do to make reporting easier?**_____

   _____

Name _____   Skill: Fiction Comprehension

Rule
Understanding what happens in a story is called **comprehension.**

Read the story, then answer the questions about it.

Luke groaned as he tried to sit up in bed. Yesterday he had been riding his bike when he fell and broke his leg. The doctor had set the bone and put on a cast. He had spent the night in the hospital, but now he was back at home. His leg was throbbing and the cast felt like it weighed a ton. Worst of all, Luke had an itch on his knee, but he couldn't reach it through the cast. Luke began to feel very sorry for himself. He would be stuck in this cast for the rest of summer vacation. What horrible luck! Even if his friends wanted to come see him, Luke wouldn't be able to do much with them.

1. **A good title for this story would be:**
   a. A Broken Leg
   b. Luke is Sick
   c. The Itchy Knee
2. **How did Luke break his leg?** _____

   _____

3. **What is a word that means "very bad"?**
   a. horrible
   b. throbbing
   c. hospital

4. **How is Luke feeling in this story? Why?** _____

   _____

5. **Name two things that are bad about the cast.** _____

   _____

6. **What would you do to cheer Luke?** _____

   _____

> **Rule**
> Understanding what happens in a story is called **comprehension.**

Read the story, then answer the questions about it.

Jackie sat quietly in the tree house. She lowered her head so she could not see over the wall and began to listen to the sounds of her neighborhood. Jackie could tell that her neighbor, Mrs. Sanders, had her kitchen window open because she could hear the sound of dishes being washed in the sink. She could hear a dog barking farther down the block. Jackie closed her eyes and listened harder. She could hear the tinkle of wind chimes and leaves rustling in the gentle breeze. She heard the buzz of a mosquito as it flitted around her head, looking for a place where it might land.

1. **A good title for this story would be:**
   a. What Jackie Saw
   b. The Sounds of the Neighborhood
   c. The Tree House
2. **Where was Jackie sitting?** _____

   _____

3. **What is a word that means "a light, ringing sound"?**
   a. gentle
   b. flitted
   c. tinkle
4. **What was Mrs. Sanders doing?** _____

   _____

5. **Why do you think Jackie "closed her eyes" to listen harder?** _____

   _____

6. **What do you think Jackie's mood is? Explain.** _____

   _____

Rule
Understanding what happens in a story is called **comprehension.**

Read the story, then answer the questions about it.

Hetty sat by herself at the corner of the playground. She felt like crying, but didn't want the other kids to see her. What a horrible morning. Melody had brought a beautiful ring to school and all the girls really liked it. Melody left it on her desk when she went to the bathroom and it was gone when she returned. Hetty sat next to Melody, and now all the girls were saying that she had stolen the ring. How could Melody think that Hetty had taken it? They were best friends and Hetty would never do something like that. The other girls were whispering and looking at Hetty now. How could she prove that she was innocent?

1. **A good title for this story would be:**
    a. Hetty is a Thief
    b. A Day at School
    c. The Missing Ring
2. **What had happened in class that morning?**_____

    _____

    3. **What is a word that means "came back"?**
    a. returned
    b. stolen
    c. playground
4. **Why did Melody think that Hetty may have taken the ring?**_____

    _____

5. **What word might describe how Hetty is feeling? Explain why.**_____

    _____

    _____

6. **What would you do if you were Hetty?**_____

    _____

Rule

Understanding what happens in a story is called **comprehension.**

Read the story, then answer the questions about it.

A community is a group of people that live in the same area. Many people live and work in your community. Early people used to live in small family groups. They produced everything from the food they ate to the clothes they wore. As people became more civilized, they began to depend on each other for their special skills. One family would make shoes and another grew crops. Families began to settle closer together and trade for the things they needed. As more families grouped together, communities were formed.

1. **A good title for this story would be:**
   a. Our Family Makes Shoes
   b. How Families Live
   c. Why We Live in Communities
2. **What groups did people live in during the early years?**_____

   _____

3. **Which word means "a group of people living and working together"?**
   a. civilized
   b. community
   c. formed
4. **Name two things from the story that people do in communities.**_____

   _____

5. **Why do you think being civilized made people need each other more?**_____

   _____

6. **Name something you think you would like to do in a community. Why?**____

   _____

   _____

> **Rule**
> Understanding what happens in a story is called **comprehension.**

Read the story, then answer the questions about it.

Language is the most important thing ever invented. Language allows us to communicate, or share information, with each other. It is what lets us share thoughts and ideas and explain how we feel or what we need. No matter what language you speak, you are communicating through words. Words are used when we talk on the phone, write a letter or telegram, listen to the radio, read a book, or watch a movie. Even people who can't hear use language to communicate. They speak with hand signals. What a lonely place this world would be without language!

1. **A good title for this story would be:**
   a. Some People Use Sign Language
   b. Language Is Important
   c. How to Write a Telegram
2. **According to this story, what is the most important invention of all?**____

   _____

3. **What is a word that means "to share information"?**
   a. language
   b. communicate
   c. signal
4. **How do people who can't hear use language?**_____

   _____

5. **Name two ways of communicating that are not listed in the story:**_____

   _____

6. **What was the last communication you had with another person?**_____

   _____

Rule

Understanding what happens in a story is called **comprehension.**

Read the story, then answer the questions about it.

From where does the milk you drink come? If your answer is, "a cow," you are probably right. However, did you know that not everyone drinks cow's milk? Children in Lapland drink milk from reindeer. In India, milk often comes from the water buffalo. Arab children like the rich, thick milk that comes from camels, and Greek children think goat's milk is the best. If you are in Tibet, you may drink a glass of yak milk. Some babies have an allergy to animal milk, and it makes them sick. They might have a bottle of milk that doesn't come from any animal at all. It is soy milk made from soybeans!

1. **A good title for this story would be:**
   a. Different Kinds of Milk
   b. Some Babies Drink Soy Milk
   c. Milk Comes from Cows

2. **What kind of milk would a Greek child drink?**_____

   _____

3. **What is a word that means "something that causes a rash or illness"?**
   a. a reindeer
   b. soybeans
   c. an allergy

4. **Name three animals in the story that give milk.**_____

   _____

5. **Why do some babies drink soy milk?**_____

   _____

6. **What type of milk would you not like to try? Why?**_____

   _____

Rule

Understanding what happens in a story is called **comprehension.**

Read the story, then answer the questions about it.

Your first name is probably the first gift you ever received from your family. You may be named after a favorite uncle or aunt. Your name may be a reminder of something that happened around the time you were born. Your name may simply be one that your parents liked. Whatever your name, it might be one that you can find anywhere in the world. The English name *John* is *Juan* in Spanish, *Johann* in German, *Ivan* in Russian, and *Sean* in Irish. The Irish *Moira*, Italian *Maria*, and French *Marie* are all the same as the English name *Mary*. Do you know what your name is in another country?

1. **A good title for this story would be:**
   a. John and Mary around the World
   b. Named after Grandfather
   c. What's in a Name?

2. **What is the English name for the French *Marie*?** _____

   _____

3. **What is a word that means "a thing to help you remember"?**
   a. Italian
   b. country
   c. reminder

4. **What is the name for *John* in Russian? In Spanish?** _____

   _____

5. **Why do you think people have first names?** _____

   _____

6. **Why did your family give you your first name?** _____

   _____

   _____

Name _____   Skill: Nonfiction Comprehension

Rule

Understanding what happens in a story is called **comprehension**.

Read the story, then answer the questions about it.

How many times have teachers told you that you weren't paying attention? Does it happen often? There are many things that affect our attention. If you haven't had enough sleep, it is hard to focus on your studies. Some children are easily distracted, or have their thoughts drawn away, by something else that is happening in the classroom. Sometimes the buzz of the lights or the grinding pencil sharpener can cause you to drift away from what the teacher is saying. You *are* paying attention, but not to the most important things. If you are easily distracted, you might try sitting closer to the front of the room near the teacher.

1. **A good title for this story would be:**
   a. Teachers are Mean
   b. Lights that Buzz
   c. Paying Attention
2. **What are two things named in the story that might be distracting?**_____

   _____

   3. **What is a word that means "to draw away attention"?**
   a. focus
   b. distract
   c. grinding
4. **Why might the teacher think a student is not paying attention?**_____

   _____

5. **What can you do to help yourself pay better attention?**_____

   _____

6. **What things in your classroom are distracting? Explain.**_____

   _____

   _____

> **Rule**
> **Letters** are messages that we write to other people or organizations.

Read the letter below, then answer the questions about it.

June 15

Dear Max,

   Next week my family is leaving for our vacation. We are going to Mount Rushmore to see the Presidents' faces on the mountain. We will be gone for two weeks.
   Would you do me a favor? My parents won't let me take Muffin with us on the trip. She can stay in her cage, but she needs to be fed and watered every day. She also needs to have her coat and long ears brushed once a week. If you will take care of her for me, I'd be very grateful. I even promise to bring you a nice gift from our travels. Please let me know if you can take care of Muffin. Thanks a lot.

Your friend,
Marvin

1. What does Marvin ask Max to do?_____

_____

2. What is a word that means "thankful"?
   a. vacation
   b. promise
   c. grateful
3. Where is Marvin's family going?_____

_____

4. What must Max do to take care of Muffin?_____

_____

5. What kind of animal do you think Muffin is? Explain why._____

_____

> **Rule**
> **Letters** are messages that we write to other people or organizations.

Read the letter below, then answer the questions about it.

February 21

Dear Mr. Piper,

   Our Boy Scout troop would like to thank you for coming to our meeting last week. We enjoyed hearing about your experiences as a sailor. It was exciting to hear your story about that big storm at sea and how it pushed your ship around. We all thought the story about the new cook and the food he made was very funny! Best of all, we enjoyed learning how to tie the knots you showed us. Our Scout Master had us practice the knots all week and will give us a test on them this Saturday.

   Thank you so much for sharing your stories and knowledge with us. Please come back and visit us again!

Sincerely,
Troop 709

1. **Why did Troop 709 write this letter to Mr. Piper?**_____

_____

2. **What is a word that means "to learn by doing something over and over"?**
   a. knots
   b. practice
   c. sharing
3. **Which story of Mr. Piper's was funny?**_____

_____

4. **On which information will the troop have a test next Saturday?**_____

_____

5. **What would you like to ask a sailor? Explain.**_____

_____

_____

Rule
Letters are messages that we write to other people or organizations.

Read the letter below, then answer the questions about it.

March 9

Dear Kim Lei,

    I told my teacher about Tet, your country's New Year celebration. She found information about your holiday and taught my whole class about it! We had a Tet party, too! We read about the dance with the dragon that chases away evil spirits. Everyone helped make a huge dragon mask, and we did the dragon dance through the halls. We also gave each other red envelopes filled with nice sayings and a little money, just as you do in your country. Our Tet celebration was not as important as yours, but we all enjoyed it and learned a lot more about your country!

                            Your pen pal,
                            Susan

1. **What is Susan telling Kim Lei in this letter?** _____

   _____

2. **What is a word that means "an occasion or event being observed"?**
   a. celebration
   b. spirits
   c. country
3. **What is the purpose of the dragon dance?** _____

   _____

4. **What did the children put into the red envelopes?** _____

   _____

5. **Is it good to learn about customs from other countries? Why or why not?**

   _____

   _____

Rule

A **noun** is a word that names a person, place, or thing. The underlined words are nouns.

The girl rode to school on the bus.

Underline every noun in each sentence.

1. An acorn will grow into an oak tree.

2. When a child grows up, she becomes an adult.

3. I need one more dime to pay for this pen.

4. The boat pulled up to the dock.

5. You need to use your brain to learn!

6. Brad is a really nice boy.

7. It is so hot, I think I will have a cold glass of lemonade.

8. The grass is getting long, so it is time to mow the lawn.

9. The soldier went to boot camp for six weeks.

10. Would you like to be my partner for the field trip?

11. Beth and Amy will work together on the report.

12. Brittney wore a hat and mittens today.

13. The large butterfly fluttered near the flowers in the garden.

14. My feet were cold after playing in the snow.

Rule

A **noun** is a word that names a person, place, or thing. The underlined words are nouns.

The girl rode to school on the bus.

Underline every noun in each sentence.

1. That book report is due Monday.

2. The headlights on that car are very bright!

3. We caught a lizard in the desert.

4. It got cold enough to leave a little frost on the grass last night.

5. The future is ahead of us!

6. That customer bought groceries today.

7. A pretty bluebird was singing in the tree.

8. The carpenter built the cupboards for Mom.

9. The bird left its footprints under the window!

10. The chickens were clucking in the barnyard.

11. Brian counted the ants as they marched across the sidewalk.

12. Do not ride a bike on busy streets!

13. Jason turned on the lights because the room was dark.

14. The baby had three stuffed animals in her crib.

> **Rule**
> A **noun** is a word that names a person, place, or thing. The underlined words are nouns.
> *The girl rode to school on the bus.*

Underline every noun in each sentence.

1. Johnny is a member of the drama club.

2. The mail carrier left a package at the door.

3. The dolphin waved his flipper as he swam away.

4. The child wore moccasins on her feet.

5. Jacob filled the tank with gas this morning.

6. The cowboys rode into the canyon.

7. My favorite fruit is the banana.

8. We roasted marshmallows over the campfire.

9. My aunt's daughter is my cousin.

10. Mrs. Greene and her husband took a trip.

11. The house on the corner has a big porch.

12. The deer ran into the forest when it heard the car coming.

13. The artist paints pictures of birds.

14. Nathan could not find his belt.

Name _____   Skill: Nouns

Rule

A **noun** is a word that names a person, place, or thing. The underlined words are nouns.

The girl rode to school on the bus.

Underline every noun in each sentence.

1. I keep sixteen goldfish in my pond.

2. Put on a sweater because it is chilly today!

3. Charlene wore a red ribbon in her hair.

4. I like to look at old photographs of people.

5. The children made puppets to put on a show at school.

6. The farmer cut the wheat in his field.

7. Jenny wrote the letter on the computer.

8. The birds sat on the ledge of the tall building.

9. The hunter had a log cabin deep in the woods.

10. The knight wore heavy armor into battle.

11. Three boys will sing this song at the concert.

12. Benjamin wore old clothes when he painted the house.

13. The box of candy costs four dollars.

14. Marvin had a sandwich and carrots for lunch.

Rule

A **verb** is a word that shows action. The underlined words are verbs.

The boy <u>ran</u> to the field to <u>play</u> soccer.

Underline every verb in each sentence.

1. I included a drink in your lunchbox.

2. This magician will amaze you with his tricks!

3. That scientist discovered and named a new star.

4. We were excited about the trip.

5. Those rocks were formed by the volcano.

6. Stacy mumbled so no one could hear her.

7. The ball was thrown into the bushes.

8. Stir the soup while I get the bowls.

9. Please repeat the directions.

10. The firefighters will rescue the kitten from the tree.

11. We laughed and cried when we saw that movie.

12. The woman wore a beautiful diamond necklace.

13. I stained my new shirt when I spilled the paint.

14. The tree swayed and bent in the strong wind.

Rule

A **verb** is a word that shows action. The underlined words are verbs.
The boy ran to the field to play soccer.

Underline every verb in each sentence.

1. Justin was so tired he yawned.

2. That watermelon weighs fifteen pounds!

3. That star twinkles brighter than the rest.

4. She received a letter today.

5. Denise pinched herself to see if she was awake.

6. He offered some candy to his friends.

7. The horse halted in front of the bridge.

8. The tiny plant froze when snow covered it.

9. The children crowded into the small room.

10. The angry bird squawked at the stranger.

11. The campfire crackled and popped cheerfully.

12. Ralph's dog barked and growled at the cat.

13. Joey likes to read books about cars.

14. Mrs. Kincaid collects dolls.

Name _____

Rule

A **verb** is a word that shows action. The underlined words are verbs.
The boy <u>ran</u> to the field to <u>play</u> soccer.

Underline every verb in each sentence.

1. Mr. Winn admired the new red car.

2. Tyrone cautiously approached the dog.

3. The birds bathed happily in the cool water.

4. Correct the answers you got wrong on this paper.

5. The doctor carefully examined the cut.

6. The woman stared at the photograph for a long time.

7. Bryan frowned when his pencil broke.

8. Honk the car horn when you are ready.

9. It is important to obey the rules.

10. Your handwriting improves with practice.

11. Sylvia drove and Carmen watched the street signs.

12. Calvin jumped when the book fell to the floor.

13. Amanda wants to buy a sweater for her friend.

14. The yellow flowers bloomed early this year.

Rule
A **verb** is a word that shows action. The underlined words are verbs.
The boy <u>ran</u> *to the field to* <u>play</u> *soccer.*

Underline every verb in each sentence.

1. The plumber will mend the broken pipe.

2. Grind the coffee beans and make a pot of coffee for me.

3. My knee jerked when you hit it.

4. It is time to harvest the pumpkins!

5. Please do not force me to say that.

6. We will decorate this room for the party.

7. Marc arrived at work at one o'clock.

8. I carved the turkey last year.

9. I am sorry to disappoint you, but we can't go now.

10. Fasten the snaps on your coat because it is cold out!

11. The cow munched on the grass in the field.

12. Justin's eyes sparkled as he told us the joke.

13. The snow fell gently on the trees and bushes.

14. The librarian frowned when she heard us talking so loudly.

Name _____   Skill: Adjectives

> **Rule**
> An **adjective** is a word that describes a noun or pronoun.
> *Playful* is an adjective that could describe the noun, *puppy*.

Read the sentences and choices below. For each sentence, write the correct adjective in the blank.

1. The _____ jewel was very expensive!

   precious   **pint**   **plank**

2. Wear a _____ coat in the rain.

   waiting   **waterproof**   **watch**

3. The _____ children played in the park.

   night   **need**   **noisy**

4. There were _____ marbles in the bag.

   forty   **flip**   **fly**

5. The _____ old man frowned.

   grumpy   **greet**   **grow**

6. That puppy has _____ fur.

   store   **sell**   **soft**

7. The _____ clown made us laugh.

   jelly   **jolly**   **jar**

8. The _____ grass looked cool and inviting.

   green   **grab**   **gain**

9. My _____ blanket feels great on cool nights.

   cloud   **cozy**   **cramp**

10. The _____ bat almost flew into a tree!

   band   **bend**   **blind**

Name _____   Skill: Adjectives

Rule
An **adjective** is a word that describes a noun or pronoun.
Playful is an adjective that could describe the noun, *puppy*.

Read the sentences and choices below. For each sentence, write the correct adjective in the blank.

1. The _____ apples made a tasty pie!
   cram   **crisp**   **cry**

2. Her _____ curls were shining in the sun.
   golden   **glad**   **grind**

3. The _____ pie was too hard to eat.
   find   **flower**   **frozen**

4. The _____ puppy whined for its mother.
   limped   **lonesome**   **lamp**

5. A _____ monkey tried to open the cage.
   call   **curious**   **crowd**

6. I was _____ before the recital.
   nervous   **nap**   **niece**

7. The puppy has _____ ears.
   floppy   **finish**   **fresh**

8. That _____ mine is too dangerous to play near.
   out   **operate**   **old**

9. The _____ road made the car bounce.
   bean   **bumpy**   **blind**

10. There were _____ girls and six boys at the party.
    elf   **ever**   **eleven**

Name _____   Skill: Adjectives

Rule

An **adjective** is a word that describes a noun or pronoun.
Playful is an adjective that could describe the noun, *puppy*.

Read the sentences and choices below. For each sentence, write the correct adjective in the blank.

1. Is your number _____ or even?

            old   odd   open

2. I would like a _____ , juicy steak.

            three   that   thick

3. Will you help me lift this _____ box?

            heavy   hold   haste

4. Otters are _____ animals.

            penny   paying   playful

5. The _____ town looked far away.

            distant   drive   drip

6. Myron was _____ to start the party.

            anxious   ants   actual

7. The _____ boy drank six glasses of water.

            think   thirty   thirsty

8. That _____ hat is beautiful!

            polite   puddle   purple

9. Jose is _____ years old.

            thirty   third   thankful

10. The cat settled down in its _____ new bed.

            snarled   snug   several

Rule

An **adjective** is a word that describes a noun or pronoun.

Playful is an adjective that could describe the noun, *puppy*.

Read the sentences and choices below. For each sentence, write the correct adjective in the blank.

1. The _____ scream upset me!

    shell   shy   shrill

2. I have _____ toes.

    ten   tank   tart

3. I have _____ sheets on my bed.

    walnut   white   worse

4. I used a _____ rag to wipe up the mess.

    damp   down   dark

5. That _____ girl knocked me down!

    red   ripe   rude

6. The _____ day made me sleepy.

    pink   plume   peaceful

7. We had a _____ time at your party!

    mashed   marvelous   modern

8. The _____ man smiled warmly at the girl.

    handsome   hook   handful

9. The _____ boy would not clean his room.

    leopard   liquid   lazy

10. A _____ bag can be very useful!

    plastic   parent   pumping

Name _____ Skill: Subject

Underline the complete subject of each sentence.

1. Mark Brown went on a trip with his family.

2. They rented a trailer and drove to California.

3. The family drove through the mountains.

4. The mountains were tall and beautiful.

5. Clouds covered the tops of the tallest mountains!

6. The Brown family also camped in a few parks.

7. Their trailer kept them safe from wild animals.

8. A bear was in their campsite one night!

9. Raccoons tried to get into the food supply.

10. The animals were never a real threat to the family, though.

11. Mark took many pictures of all the things they saw.

12. The pictures were a good reminder of that wonderful trip.

Write your own subject for each sentence.

1. _____ ate cookies and ice cream.

2. _____ swam in the pool.

3. _____ will take us to school.

4. _____ watched the baby.

Rule

The **simple subject** is a noun or pronoun that tells whom or what the sentence is about.

The **complete subject** includes the simple subject and all the words that tell more about it.

The white cat slept on the pillow.

The simple subject is *cat* and the complete subject is *The white cat*.

Underline the complete subject of each sentence.

1. A noun is a person, place, or thing.

2. Verbs are words that show action or being.

3. People use nouns and verbs together to make sentences.

4. Adjectives can be used to tell more about nouns or pronouns.

5. Adverbs tell more about the verb.

6. A sentence tells a complete thought.

7. A sentence only needs a subject and a predicate.

8. The subject is the noun that the sentence is about.

9. The predicate tells what the subject is doing.

10. Other words in the sentence tell more about the subject and predicate.

11. You can find the subject if you try.

12. It isn't very hard to do!

Write your own subject for each sentence.

1. _____ went to the movie.

2. _____ plays the drums in the band.

3. _____ understands that story.

4. _____ is a very nice person.

> **Rule**
> The **simple subject** is a noun or pronoun that tells whom or what the sentence is about.
> The **complete subject** includes the simple subject and all the words that tell more about it.
> *The white cat slept on the pillow.*
> The simple subject is *cat* and the complete subject is *The white ca*t.

Underline the complete subject of each sentence.

1. Africa is one of the continents of the Earth.

2. Africa has many different countries.

3. Kenya is a country in eastern Africa.

4. The southeast coast of Africa borders the Indian Ocean.

5. Kenya has a famous park.

6. Mt. Elgon National Park is the name of the park.

7. It is a great place to watch elephants.

8. Large lions live there, too.

9. Many visitors come to see the animals each year.

10. A hotel was built near a watering hole for the animals.

11. People can watch the wild animals right from their rooms!

12. The animals like to watch the people, too!

Write your own subject for each sentence.

1. _____ is my favorite pet.

2. _____ ate pickles and peanut butter.

3. _____ like to listen to music.

4. _____ rode the wagon to town.

Rule

The **simple subject** is a noun or pronoun that tells whom or what the sentence is about.

The **complete subject** includes the simple subject and all the words that tell more about it.

The white cat slept on the pillow.
The simple subject is *cat* and the complete subject is *The white cat*.

Underline the complete subject of each sentence.

1. Susan plays flute in the school band.

2. Two mice stored seeds in the garden.

3. Chess is my favorite game.

4. The leaves on the trees are turning color.

5. Janice read a book that was funny.

6. Those brown socks do not match your pants.

7. Carol lost her sweater at the party.

8. The Rodriguez family has a yellow van.

9. Penny went to the park with her friends after school.

10. That science project is the best one in third grade!

11. The brown and white horse is running across the field.

12. The rain fell all afternoon.

Write your own subject for each sentence.

1. _____ bought a new pair of skates.

2. _____ ate at a restaurant.

3. _____ washed its paws in the river.

4. _____ was speeding down the street.

Name _____   Skill: Predicate

Rule

The **simple predicate** is a verb that tells what the subject did or what was done to the subject.

The **complete predicate** includes the verb and all the words that tell more about it.

The white cat slept on the pillow.

The simple predicate is *slept* and the complete predicate is *slept on the pillow.*

Underline the complete predicate of each sentence.

1. The cows and horses stayed in the barn during the storm.

2. The small brown fox ran into the hole.

3. Alex and his brother played all afternoon.

4. Uncle Vinnie sent a postcard from Italy.

5. My mother and father are going to the store.

6. The large, green truck rolled down the highway.

7. It was snowing last week.

8. My sister baby-sits for the neighbors.

9. We will eat dinner.

10. I danced in the play.

11. The oranges and lemons grew in the orchard.

12. Rusty and Terry took the test yesterday.

Write your own predicate for each sentence.

1. Jonas and Kristie _____ .

2. Those rabbits _____ .

3. The desk in the front row _____ .

4. All of the children _____ .

Rule

The **simple predicate** is a verb that tells what the subject did or what was done to the subject.

The **complete predicate** includes the verb and all the words that tell more about it.

The white cat slept on the pillow.

The simple predicate is *slept* and the complete predicate is *slept on the pillow.*

Underline the complete predicate of each sentence.

1. I like the colors yellow and blue.

2. My teacher, Miss Winter, brought a gerbil for the class.

3. Kevin wants to be a doctor someday.

4. The telephone rang seven times!

5. That little boy lost his shoe this morning.

6. Mike cut his hair very short.

7. The thief stole the diamond necklace.

8. The big brown bear protected her cub.

9. The audience clapped at the end of the play.

10. My mother writes books.

11. The man with the beard drives a truck.

12. Brian held the baby bird.

Write your own predicate for each sentence.

1. The big brown box _____ .

2. Six boys _____ .

3. My younger brother _____ .

4. When you smile, you _____ .

Rule

A **simple predicate** is a verb that tells what the subject did or what was done to the subject.

A **complete predicate** includes the verb and all the words that tell more about it.

The white cat slept on the pillow.

The simple predicate is *slept* and the complete predicate is *slept on the pillow*.

Underline the complete predicate of each sentence.

1. The marching band plays in every parade.

2. I watched television until bedtime.

3. The sad little girl cried.

4. Lamont jumped over the fence.

5. The airplane landed in Chicago.

6. The boat with the blue sails tipped over in the storm.

7. Liz covered her head during the scary part of the movie.

8. That photographer takes great pictures!

9. The wind blew over the picnic table.

10. We built a sand castle at the beach.

11. We ate lots of ice cream.

12. Ben walks to school.

Write your own predicate for each sentence.

1. Before school I _____ .

2. The zebras and monkeys _____ .

3. My class _____ .

4. The computer in the office _____ .

Rule
A **simple predicate** is a verb that tells what the subject did or what was done to the subject.
A **complete predicate** includes the verb and all the words that tell more about it.
The white cat slept on the pillow.
The simple predicate is *slept* and the complete predicate is *slept on the pillow*.

Underline the complete predicate of each sentence.

1. Pamela will write six letters tonight.

2. The kitten hides under the couch.

3. My best friend moved to another state.

4. The wild animals roamed the forest.

5. Jerry enjoyed the movie.

6. Randy and Karl swim in the lake.

7. My aunt's pizza tastes wonderful!

8. The two friends sat together on the bus.

9. George picked blueberries yesterday.

10. My dad built my tree house.

11. The yellow and white daisies swayed in the breeze.

12. Carlos saw the accident last week.

Write your own predicate for each sentence.

1. Brittany's cat _____ .

2. My elbow _____ .

3. The package with the green bow _____ .

4. The mail carrier _____ .

Rule

A **sentence** is a group of words that expresses a complete thought.

A **fragment** is an incomplete sentence because it does not express a complete thought.

Fragments: *Anna and Beth.* (missing a predicate that tells what happened)

                Went swimming. (missing a subject that tells who)

Sentence: *Anna and Beth went swimming.*

Write **S** if the words below form a sentence and **F** if they are a fragment.

_____ 1. The picture on the wall.

_____ 2. We rented skates.

_____ 3. Bowling in the afternoon.

_____ 4. The curious little kitten.

_____ 5. Keep the cookies separate from the doughnuts.

_____ 6. Alice and Glenda wrote the play.

_____ 7. Acted as if they were really scared.

_____ 8. The panda ate bamboo shoots.

_____ 9. Pedro and his cousin, Juan.

_____ 10. Running through the neighbor's yard.

_____ 11. The big moving van came down our street.

_____ 12. Called hello to all our friends.

Add words to make each fragment a sentence.

1. Storms are _____ .

2. _____ racing each other.

3. A very loud noise _____ .

4. _____ playing in the warm sunshine.

Skill: Fragments

Rule

A **sentence** is a group of words that expresses a complete thought.
A **fragment** is an incomplete sentence because it does not express a complete thought.

Fragments: *Anna and Beth.* (missing a predicate that tells what happened)
Went swimming. (missing a subject that tells who)

Sentence: *Anna and Beth went swimming.*

Write **S** if the words below form a sentence and **F** if they are a fragment.

_____ 1. The moment we have been waiting for.

_____ 2. The queen's gown was lovely.

_____ 3. Across the street and in the yard.

_____ 4. Albert waited quietly.

_____ 5. The Empire State Building and other buildings.

_____ 6. Perhaps after dinner.

_____ 7. We held our breath and waited for the answer.

_____ 8. A wild look in his eyes.

_____ 9. Miguel hid behind the tree.

_____ 10. The nicest looking cake I had ever seen.

_____ 11. Through the fields and into the barnyard.

_____ 12. Francine waved to us.

Add words to make each fragment a sentence.

1. From the front of the boat _____ .

2. _____ eating grapes.

3. The whole group _____ .

4. _____ picking flowers.

Rule
Remember to use **capital letters** for:
- the first word in a sentence   • the pronoun "I"
- proper nouns   • important words in book and movie titles

Each sentence below has one or more capitalization mistakes. Write each sentence correctly on the line below it.

1. My uncle's name is edward.

_____

2. the line for the movie was very long.

_____

3. Huey and i are best friends.

_____

4. We will study the country of ireland.

_____

5. I am reading a book called <u>the little prince</u>.

_____

6. Lucille and margaret brought flowers.

_____

7. James just got back from florida.

_____

8. The name of my doctor is paula milne.

_____

9. we can play after school.

_____

10. The nile river is the longest river in the world.

_____

11. The teacher just finished reading <u>charlotte's web</u>.

_____

12. joey went to texas last summer.

_____

Rule

Remember to use **capital letters** for:
   • the first word in a sentence   • the pronoun "I"
   • proper nouns   • important words in book and movie titles

Each sentence below has one or more capitalization mistakes. Write each sentence correctly on the line below it.

1. the ugly duckling is my favorite fairy tale.

   _____

2. when i clap my hands, we will line up.

   _____

3. I like to go shopping with maude and kathy.

   _____

4. Have you ever been to africa?

   _____

5. My dad just read a novel called <u>treasure island</u>.

   _____

6. i would like to visit france some day.

   _____

7. We flew to new york for thanksgiving.

   _____

8. mexico is a country in north america.

   _____

9. the baseball broke the window.

   _____

10. We took a trip to california last august.

   _____

11. My birthday is on tuesday this year.

   _____

12. It often snows in december.

   _____

Name _____   Skill: Addition Facts

Add.

1. 3
    + 2

2. 7
    + 0

3. 9
    + 4

4. 3
    + 7

5. 8
    + 8

6. 5
    + 2

7. 4
    + 7

8. 1
    + 2

9. 4
    + 7

10. 3
    + 4

11. 5
    + 9

12. 9
    + 8

13. 2
    + 1

14. 8
    + 3

15. 0
    + 9

16. 6
    + 5

17. 8
    + 5

18. 4
    + 7

19. 2
    + 2

20. 5
    + 3

21. 3
    + 8

22. 8
    + 0

23. 7
    + 4

24. 4
    + 5

25. 1
    + 9

26. 9
    + 7

27. 5
    + 3

28. 3
    + 6

29. 6
    + 4

30. 9
    + 9

31. 8
    + 8

32. 3
    + 3

33. 8
    + 2

34. 2
    + 1

35. 7
    + 6

36. 10
    + 2

37. 0
    + 9

38. 2
    + 0

39. 6
    + 5

40. 4
    + 1

41. 9
    + 7

42. 7
    + 3

43. 6
    + 9

44. 7
    + 6

45. 9
    + 6

46. 6
    + 2

47. 5
    + 5

48. 5
    + 4

49. 10
    + 1

Name _____   Skill: Two-Digit Addition

Add.

1. 33
  + 21

2. 70
  + 20

3. 39
  + 40

4. 31
  + 57

5. 28
  + 11

6. 56
  + 23

7. 44
  + 23

8. 71
  + 25

9. 42
  + 47

10. 63
  + 14

11. 50
  + 17

12. 29
  + 70

13. 82
  + 16

14. 38
  + 31

15. 70
  + 19

16. 46
  + 12

17. 70
  + 14

18. 54
  + 14

19. 20
  + 30

20. 25
  + 34

21. 53
  + 16

22. 28
  + 50

23. 17
  + 42

24. 24
  + 50

25. 81
  + 11

26. 33
  + 23

27. 51
  + 35

28. 13
  + 66

29. 56
  + 41

30. 19
  + 70

31. 34
  + 12

32. 13
  + 43

33. 58
  + 20

34. 23
  + 25

35. 47
  + 22

36. 10
  + 24

37. 37
  + 20

38. 26
  + 43

39. 61
  + 17

40. 44
  + 34

41. 29
  + 40

42. 72
  + 13

43. 60
  + 29

44. 57
  + 11

45. 49
  + 50

46. 26
  + 20

47. 52
  + 25

48. 53
  + 41

49. 35
  + 21

Name _____

Add.

1. 53 + 29	2. 17 + 55	3. 46 + 27	4. 38 + 49	5. 45 + 28	6. 86 + 64	7. 27 + 39
8. 99 + 59	9. 23 + 78	10. 38 + 57	11. 85 + 53	12. 91 + 46	13. 33 + 19	14. 84 + 37
15. 29 + 61	16. 92 + 48	17. 22 + 89	18. 45 + 73	19. 74 + 18	20. 96 + 33	21. 26 + 77
22. 96 + 58	23. 26 + 86	24. 74 + 38	25. 82 + 24	26. 99 + 47	27. 46 + 28	28. 76 + 25
29. 19 + 41	30. 58 + 63	31. 63 + 59	32. 81 + 73	33. 72 + 28	34. 35 + 66	35. 27 + 28
36. 48 + 57	37. 74 + 63	38. 61 + 56	39. 70 + 54	40. 93 + 28	41. 65 + 49	42. 29 + 79
43. 36 + 77	44. 77 + 34	45. 84 + 63	46. 25 + 57	47. 89 + 21	48. 58 + 47	49. 34 + 48

Add.

1. 303 + 214	**2.** 870 + 189	**3.** 408 + 159	**4.** 327 + 196	**5.** 417 + 125	**6.** 730 + 197	**7.** 344 + 523
8. 751 + 225	**9.** 400 + 127	**10.** 111 + 345	**11.** 250 + 178	**12.** 219 + 470	**13.** 382 + 160	**14.** 348 + 436
15. 709 + 189	**16.** 522 + 157	**17.** 398 + 145	**18.** 270 + 134	**19.** 520 + 177	**20.** 254 + 384	**21.** 953 + 119
22. 428 + 150	**23.** 197 + 402	**24.** 724 + 150	**25.** 181 + 199	**26.** 533 + 238	**27.** 451 + 315	**28.** 613 + 178
29. 357 + 417	**30.** 519 + 170	**31.** 834 + 196	**32.** 313 + 488	**33.** 558 + 184	**34.** 687 + 139	**35.** 901 + 149
36. 410 + 291	**37.** 737 + 288	**38.** 426 + 497	**39.** 166 + 617	**40.** 404 + 395	**41.** 259 + 450	**42.** 272 + 438
43. 106 + 329	**44.** 857 + 241	**45.** 849 + 154	**46.** 426 + 208	**47.** 572 + 259	**48.** 553 + 347	**49.** 436 + 574

Name _____   Skill: Subtraction Facts

Subtract.

1. $\begin{array}{r} 3 \\ -2 \\ \hline \end{array}$
2. $\begin{array}{r} 7 \\ -0 \\ \hline \end{array}$
3. $\begin{array}{r} 9 \\ -4 \\ \hline \end{array}$
4. $\begin{array}{r} 7 \\ -3 \\ \hline \end{array}$
5. $\begin{array}{r} 8 \\ -8 \\ \hline \end{array}$
6. $\begin{array}{r} 5 \\ -2 \\ \hline \end{array}$
7. $\begin{array}{r} 9 \\ -4 \\ \hline \end{array}$

8. $\begin{array}{r} 4 \\ -2 \\ \hline \end{array}$
9. $\begin{array}{r} 9 \\ -7 \\ \hline \end{array}$
10. $\begin{array}{r} 10 \\ -4 \\ \hline \end{array}$
11. $\begin{array}{r} 6 \\ -1 \\ \hline \end{array}$
12. $\begin{array}{r} 9 \\ -8 \\ \hline \end{array}$
13. $\begin{array}{r} 2 \\ -1 \\ \hline \end{array}$
14. $\begin{array}{r} 8 \\ -3 \\ \hline \end{array}$

15. $\begin{array}{r} 10 \\ -9 \\ \hline \end{array}$
16. $\begin{array}{r} 12 \\ -5 \\ \hline \end{array}$
17. $\begin{array}{r} 11 \\ -4 \\ \hline \end{array}$
18. $\begin{array}{r} 10 \\ -7 \\ \hline \end{array}$
19. $\begin{array}{r} 2 \\ -2 \\ \hline \end{array}$
20. $\begin{array}{r} 15 \\ -6 \\ \hline \end{array}$
21. $\begin{array}{r} 13 \\ -8 \\ \hline \end{array}$

22. $\begin{array}{r} 8 \\ -4 \\ \hline \end{array}$
23. $\begin{array}{r} 7 \\ -2 \\ \hline \end{array}$
24. $\begin{array}{r} 14 \\ -5 \\ \hline \end{array}$
25. $\begin{array}{r} 11 \\ -9 \\ \hline \end{array}$
26. $\begin{array}{r} 17 \\ -9 \\ \hline \end{array}$
27. $\begin{array}{r} 5 \\ -3 \\ \hline \end{array}$
28. $\begin{array}{r} 13 \\ -6 \\ \hline \end{array}$

29. $\begin{array}{r} 14 \\ -6 \\ \hline \end{array}$
30. $\begin{array}{r} 9 \\ -9 \\ \hline \end{array}$
31. $\begin{array}{r} 14 \\ -7 \\ \hline \end{array}$
32. $\begin{array}{r} 13 \\ -9 \\ \hline \end{array}$
33. $\begin{array}{r} 8 \\ -2 \\ \hline \end{array}$
34. $\begin{array}{r} 12 \\ -9 \\ \hline \end{array}$
35. $\begin{array}{r} 16 \\ -7 \\ \hline \end{array}$

36. $\begin{array}{r} 10 \\ -2 \\ \hline \end{array}$
37. $\begin{array}{r} 18 \\ -9 \\ \hline \end{array}$
38. $\begin{array}{r} 12 \\ -5 \\ \hline \end{array}$
39. $\begin{array}{r} 16 \\ -7 \\ \hline \end{array}$
40. $\begin{array}{r} 14 \\ -5 \\ \hline \end{array}$
41. $\begin{array}{r} 9 \\ -7 \\ \hline \end{array}$
42. $\begin{array}{r} 17 \\ -8 \\ \hline \end{array}$

43. $\begin{array}{r} 10 \\ -6 \\ \hline \end{array}$
44. $\begin{array}{r} 7 \\ -6 \\ \hline \end{array}$
45. $\begin{array}{r} 9 \\ -6 \\ \hline \end{array}$
46. $\begin{array}{r} 6 \\ -2 \\ \hline \end{array}$
47. $\begin{array}{r} 15 \\ -8 \\ \hline \end{array}$
48. $\begin{array}{r} 17 \\ -9 \\ \hline \end{array}$
49. $\begin{array}{r} 11 \\ -6 \\ \hline \end{array}$

Name _____   Skill: Two-Digit Subtraction

Subtract.

1. 30 − 10	2. 70 − 40	3. 90 − 40	4. 60 − 30	5. 80 − 80	6. 50 − 20	7. 90 − 10
8. 40 − 20	9. 90 − 70	10. 50 − 40	11. 60 − 10	12. 90 − 80	13. 20 − 10	14. 80 − 30
15. 55 − 43	16. 72 − 50	17. 88 − 41	18. 33 − 22	19. 72 − 32	20. 75 − 64	21. 99 − 48
22. 87 − 46	23. 78 − 24	24. 83 − 51	25. 69 − 19	26. 76 − 45	27. 58 − 30	28. 66 − 62
29. 72 − 61	30. 98 − 46	31. 33 − 12	32. 84 − 23	33. 88 − 72	34. 48 − 32	35. 76 − 51
36. 95 − 23	37. 80 − 40	38. 67 − 51	39. 82 − 70	40. 96 − 53	41. 79 − 17	42. 87 − 47
43. 85 − 60	44. 70 − 60	45. 93 − 60	46. 57 − 23	47. 77 − 17	48. 84 − 62	49. 56 − 41

74

Name _____   Skill: Two-Digit Subtraction

Subtract.

1. $\begin{array}{r} 91 \\ -\ 56 \\ \hline \end{array}$
2. $\begin{array}{r} 52 \\ -\ 49 \\ \hline \end{array}$
3. $\begin{array}{r} 43 \\ -\ 38 \\ \hline \end{array}$
4. $\begin{array}{r} 71 \\ -\ 34 \\ \hline \end{array}$
5. $\begin{array}{r} 75 \\ -\ 46 \\ \hline \end{array}$
6. $\begin{array}{r} 84 \\ -\ 47 \\ \hline \end{array}$
7. $\begin{array}{r} 61 \\ -\ 12 \\ \hline \end{array}$

8. $\begin{array}{r} 86 \\ -\ 58 \\ \hline \end{array}$
9. $\begin{array}{r} 90 \\ -\ 29 \\ \hline \end{array}$
10. $\begin{array}{r} 42 \\ -\ 28 \\ \hline \end{array}$
11. $\begin{array}{r} 94 \\ -\ 66 \\ \hline \end{array}$
12. $\begin{array}{r} 62 \\ -\ 49 \\ \hline \end{array}$
13. $\begin{array}{r} 55 \\ -\ 17 \\ \hline \end{array}$
14. $\begin{array}{r} 41 \\ -\ 25 \\ \hline \end{array}$

15. $\begin{array}{r} 86 \\ -\ 39 \\ \hline \end{array}$
16. $\begin{array}{r} 34 \\ -\ 18 \\ \hline \end{array}$
17. $\begin{array}{r} 73 \\ -\ 38 \\ \hline \end{array}$
18. $\begin{array}{r} 44 \\ -\ 15 \\ \hline \end{array}$
19. $\begin{array}{r} 73 \\ -\ 25 \\ \hline \end{array}$
20. $\begin{array}{r} 58 \\ -\ 39 \\ \hline \end{array}$
21. $\begin{array}{r} 52 \\ -\ 24 \\ \hline \end{array}$

22. $\begin{array}{r} 38 \\ -\ 19 \\ \hline \end{array}$
23. $\begin{array}{r} 46 \\ -\ 28 \\ \hline \end{array}$
24. $\begin{array}{r} 53 \\ -\ 28 \\ \hline \end{array}$
25. $\begin{array}{r} 95 \\ -\ 48 \\ \hline \end{array}$
26. $\begin{array}{r} 84 \\ -\ 27 \\ \hline \end{array}$
27. $\begin{array}{r} 64 \\ -\ 39 \\ \hline \end{array}$
28. $\begin{array}{r} 92 \\ -\ 59 \\ \hline \end{array}$

29. $\begin{array}{r} 87 \\ -\ 38 \\ \hline \end{array}$
30. $\begin{array}{r} 74 \\ -\ 25 \\ \hline \end{array}$
31. $\begin{array}{r} 67 \\ -\ 38 \\ \hline \end{array}$
32. $\begin{array}{r} 71 \\ -\ 64 \\ \hline \end{array}$
33. $\begin{array}{r} 83 \\ -\ 28 \\ \hline \end{array}$
34. $\begin{array}{r} 41 \\ -\ 34 \\ \hline \end{array}$
35. $\begin{array}{r} 71 \\ -\ 42 \\ \hline \end{array}$

36. $\begin{array}{r} 93 \\ -\ 75 \\ \hline \end{array}$
37. $\begin{array}{r} 84 \\ -\ 19 \\ \hline \end{array}$
38. $\begin{array}{r} 82 \\ -\ 73 \\ \hline \end{array}$
39. $\begin{array}{r} 84 \\ -\ 37 \\ \hline \end{array}$
40. $\begin{array}{r} 66 \\ -\ 48 \\ \hline \end{array}$
41. $\begin{array}{r} 75 \\ -\ 27 \\ \hline \end{array}$
42. $\begin{array}{r} 54 \\ -\ 39 \\ \hline \end{array}$

43. $\begin{array}{r} 75 \\ -\ 17 \\ \hline \end{array}$
44. $\begin{array}{r} 47 \\ -\ 18 \\ \hline \end{array}$
45. $\begin{array}{r} 40 \\ -\ 29 \\ \hline \end{array}$
46. $\begin{array}{r} 61 \\ -\ 23 \\ \hline \end{array}$
47. $\begin{array}{r} 54 \\ -\ 38 \\ \hline \end{array}$
48. $\begin{array}{r} 81 \\ -\ 27 \\ \hline \end{array}$
49. $\begin{array}{r} 93 \\ -\ 56 \\ \hline \end{array}$

Subtract.

1. 326
   − 285

2. 972
   − 609

3. 685
   − 246

4. 518
   − 329

5. 741
   − 362

6. 438
   − 258

7. 371
   − 283

8. 529
   − 482

9. 625
   − 407

10. 514
    − 126

11. 664
    − 278

12. 742
    − 467

13. 200
    − 158

14. 634
    − 277

15. 423
    − 285

16. 222
    − 153

17. 435
    − 166

18. 628
    − 499

19. 757
    − 178

20. 637
    − 388

21. 423
    − 285

22. 533
    − 240

23. 415
    − 196

24. 382
    − 175

25. 632
    − 377

26. 585
    − 423

27. 778
    − 439

28. 165
    −130

29. 623
    − 194

30. 900
    − 309

31. 722
    − 317

32. 377
    − 186

33. 871
    − 384

34. 628
    − 300

35. 454
    − 279

36. 990
    − 731

37. 818
    − 693

38. 572
    − 335

39. 951
     357

40. 825
    − 469

41. 771
    − 217

42. 943
    − 761

43. 407
    − 328

44. 431
    − 298

45. 906
    − 682

46. 486
    − 297

47. 615
    − 288

48. 883
    − 227

49. 725
    − 387

Name _____   Skill: Multiplication Facts

Multiply.

1.	2.	3.	4.	5.	6.	7.
3 x 2	7 x 0	9 x 3	3 x 1	8 x 2	5 x 2	3 x 7

8.	9.	10.	11.	12.	13.	14.
1 x 2	0 x 8	3 x 4	2 x 9	9 x 0	2 x 1	8 x 3

15.	16.	17.	18.	19.	20.	21.
9 x 1	6 x 3	0 x 4	5 x 1	2 x 2	5 x 3	3 x 2

22.	23.	24.	25.	26.	27.	28.
8 x 0	8 x 3	1 x 5	3 x 9	9 x 2	5 x 0	3 x 6

29.	30.	31.	32.	33.	34.	35.
6 x 0	9 x 3	1 x 7	3 x 3	8 x 2	2 x 1	7 x 2

36.	37.	38.	39.	40.	41.	42.
10 x 2	0 x 9	2 x 0	3 x 5	0 x 1	9 x 3	8 x 2

43.	44.	45.	46.	47.	48.	49.
6 x 3	7 x 1	2 x 6	4 x 2	5 x 0	1 x 4	2 x 9

Name _____   Skill: Multiplication Facts

Multiply.

1. 3   2. 7   3. 6   4. 3   5. 8   6. 4   7. 3
   x 4   x 5   x 3   x 7   x 5   x 2   x 6

8. 1   9. 0   10. 6   11. 7   12. 9   13. 5   14. 8
   x 4   x 5   x 4   x 9   x 4   x 1   x 6

15. 9   16. 6   17. 0   18. 5   19. 4   20. 5   21. 3
   x 4   x 5   x 6   x 7   x 2   x 5   x 6

22. 8   23. 8   24. 1   25. 6   26. 9   27. 5   28. 6
   x 7   x 4   x 5   x 9   x 7   x 4   x 6

29. 6   30. 9   31. 4   32. 3   33. 8   34. 2   35. 7
   x 6   x 5   x 7   x 7   x 5   x 4   x 7

36. 10   37. 4   38. 5   39. 8   40. 6   41. 9   42. 7
   x 4   x 1   x 0   x 5   x 1   x 6   x 9

43. 6   44. 7   45. 7   46. 5   47. 5   48. 7   49. 2
   x 7   x 7   x 6   x 2   x 6   x 4   x 8

Multiply.

1. 8 x 3	**2.** 7 x 9	**3.** 10 x 3	**4.** 11 x 3	**5.** 8 x 8	**6.** 9 x 2	**7.** 10 x 7
8. 12 x 2	**9.** 10 x 8	**10.** 9 x 4	**11.** 8 x 9	**12.** 10 x 9	**13.** 12 x 1	**14.** 8 x 3
15. 12 x 9	**16.** 6 x 9	**17.** 10 x 4	**18.** 12 x 5	**19.** 10 x 2	**20.** 8 x 3	**21.** 9 x 8
22. 11 x 0	**23.** 8 x 3	**24.** 12 x 5	**25.** 7 x 8	**26.** 9 x 9	**27.** 10 x 3	**28.** 11 x 6
29. 10 x 6	**30.** 9 x 3	**31.** 11 x 7	**32.** 3 x 8	**33.** 8 x 8	**34.** 10 x 2	**35.** 7 x 9
36. 11 x 2	**37.** 10 x 9	**38.** 2 x 9	**39.** 8 x 5	**40.** 10 x 1	**41.** 11 x 9	**42.** 10 x 7
43. 11 x 6	**44.** 7 x 8	**45.** 10 x 6	**46.** 12 x 6	**47.** 5 x 9	**48.** 9 x 4	**49.** 10 x 8

Divide.

1.   2.   3.   4.   5.
2⟌18   3⟌9   3⟌24   1⟌4   2⟌8

6.   7.   8.   9.   10.
3⟌15   4⟌32   1⟌12   3⟌3   2⟌20

11.   12.   13.   14.   15.
4⟌16   3⟌36   1⟌2   4⟌44   2⟌2

16.   17.   18.   19.   20.
1⟌8   2⟌6   3⟌21   4⟌12   3⟌27

21.   22.   23.   24.   25.
4⟌8   1⟌10   2⟌24   2⟌4   3⟌30

26.   27.   28.   29.   30.
3⟌12   2⟌14   1⟌9   4⟌4   3⟌33

Divide.

1. $5\overline{)15}$	**2.** $6\overline{)42}$	**3.** $7\overline{)7}$	**4.** $6\overline{)12}$	**5.** $8\overline{)96}$
6. $5\overline{)30}$	**7.** $7\overline{)35}$	**8.** $5\overline{)40}$	**9.** $8\overline{)24}$	**10.** $6\overline{)60}$
11. $6\overline{)18}$	**12.** $7\overline{)63}$	**13.** $5\overline{)5}$	**14.** $8\overline{)72}$	**15.** $6\overline{)36}$
16. $8\overline{)80}$	**17.** $5\overline{)60}$	**18.** $7\overline{)28}$	**19.** $6\overline{)66}$	**20.** $7\overline{)14}$
21. $5\overline{)35}$	**22.** $6\overline{)6}$	**23.** $8\overline{)48}$	**24.** $5\overline{)50}$	**25.** $8\overline{)88}$
26. $7\overline{)77}$	**27.** $8\overline{)32}$	**28.** $5\overline{)50}$	**29.** $8\overline{)40}$	**30.** $6\overline{)42}$

Divide.

1.
9⟌90

2.
10⟌20

3.
11⟌99

4.
12⟌108

5.
11⟌77

6.
12⟌24

7.
10⟌60

8.
12⟌60

9.
11⟌110

10.
10⟌100

11.
9⟌18

12.
12⟌72

13.
10⟌50

14.
12⟌12

15.
11⟌33

16.
9⟌27

17.
9⟌9

18.
10⟌120

19.
11⟌121

20.
9⟌108

21.
9⟌36

22.
10⟌40

23.
12⟌36

24.
11⟌22

25.
9⟌45

26.
12⟌48

27.
10⟌70

28.
9⟌63

29.
11⟌132

30.
12⟌96

Name _____   Skill: Place Value

Use the clues to find the number. Write the number. The first one has been done for you.

1. I am a number with a 4 in the ones place, a 2 in the tens place, a 6 in the hundreds place, and a 5 in the thousands place. What number am I?

$\dfrac{5}{T},\dfrac{6}{H}\ \dfrac{2}{T}\ \dfrac{4}{O}$

2. I am a number with a 9 in the tens place, a 3 in the ones place, a 2 in the thousands place, and a 6 in the hundreds place. What number am I?

$\dfrac{}{T},\dfrac{}{H}\ \dfrac{}{T}\ \dfrac{}{O}$

3. I am a number with a 7 in the hundreds place, a 1 in the tens place, a 0 in the ones place, and a 1 in the thousands place. What number am I?

$\dfrac{}{T},\dfrac{}{H}\ \dfrac{}{T}\ \dfrac{}{O}$

4. I am a number with a 5 in the ones place, a 3 in the tens place, an 8 in the hundreds place, and a 9 in the thousands place. What number am I?

$\dfrac{}{T},\dfrac{}{H}\ \dfrac{}{T}\ \dfrac{}{O}$

5. I am a number with a 4 in the thousands place, a 6 in the ones place, a 9 in the tens place, and a 5 in the hundreds place. What number am I?

$\dfrac{}{T},\dfrac{}{H}\ \dfrac{}{T}\ \dfrac{}{O}$

6. I am a number with a 1 in the tens place, a 2 in the ones place, a 3 in the hundreds place, and a 4 in the thousands place. What number am I?

$\dfrac{}{T},\dfrac{}{H}\ \dfrac{}{T}\ \dfrac{}{O}$

7. I am a number with a 7 in the ones place, a 5 in the tens place, a 3 in the thousands place, and an 8 in the hundreds place. What number am I?

$\dfrac{}{T},\dfrac{}{H}\ \dfrac{}{T}\ \dfrac{}{O}$

8. I am a number with a 0 in the hundreds place, a 3 in the ones place, a 7 in the thousands place, and an 8 in the tens place. What number am I?

$\dfrac{}{T},\dfrac{}{H}\ \dfrac{}{T}\ \dfrac{}{O}$

Answer the questions below. The first one has been done for you.

1. What number is shown?

tens	ones

_____ 74

2. What number is shown?

tens	ones

_____

3. What number is shown?

tens	ones

_____

4. What number is shown?

tens	ones

_____

5. What number is shown?

tens	ones

_____

6. What number is shown?

tens	ones

_____

7. What number is shown?

tens	ones

_____

8. What number is shown?

tens	ones

_____

Name _____   Skill: Rounding

1. Round these numbers to the nearest ten. The first one has been done for you.

a. 57 _____60_____   f. 32 _____

b. 83 _____   g. 29 _____

c. 145 _____   h. 187 _____

d. 231 _____   i. 356 _____

e. 672 _____   j. 705 _____

2. Round these numbers to the nearest hundred. The first one has been done for you.

a. 149 _____100_____   k. 739 _____

b. 391 _____   l. 299 _____

c. 651 _____   m. 807 _____

d. 1,299 _____   n. 5,356 _____

e. 3,602 _____   o. 4,725 _____

f. 893 _____   p. 99 _____

g. 4,409 _____   q. 472 _____

h. 1,560 _____   r. 3,099 _____

i. 1,929 _____   s. 1,187 _____

j. 1,499 _____   t. 1,702 _____

3. Round these numbers to the nearest thousand. The first one has been done for you.

a. 4,082 _____4,000_____   f. 3,601 _____

b. 9,429 _____   g. 1,290 _____

c. 6,900 _____   h. 7,318 _____

d. 12,195 _____   i. 13,812 _____

e. 10,500 _____   j. 15,629 _____

Name _____ Skill: Rounding

1. Round these numbers to the nearest ten. The first one has been done for you.

a. 9 _____10_____   **f.** 18 _____

b. 41 _____   **g.** 54 _____

c. 89 _____   **h.** 65 _____

d. 321 _____   **i.** 209 _____

e. 856 _____   **j.** 697 _____

2. Round these numbers to the nearest hundred. The first one has been done for you.

a. 72 _____100_____   **k.** 48 _____

b. 39 _____   **l.** 132 _____

c. 338 _____   **m.** 511 _____

d. 691 _____   **n.** 470 _____

e. 845 _____   **o.** 3,281 _____

f. 743 _____   **p.** 835 _____

g. 967 _____   **q.** 948 _____

h. 4,821 _____   **r.** 8,127 _____

i. 7,189 _____   **s.** 6,711 _____

j. 3,807 _____   **t.** 11,523 _____

3. Round these numbers to the nearest thousand. The first one has been done for you.

a. 679 _____1,000_____   **f.** 823 _____

b. 1,089 _____   **g.** 2,650 _____

c. 3,427 _____   **h.** 6,997 _____

d. 8,951 _____   **i.** 10,503 _____

e. 23,734 _____   **j.** 35,092 _____

Answer the questions. The first one has been done for you.

1. What fraction is shaded?

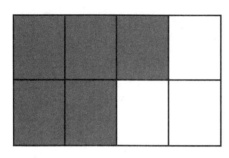

$$\frac{5}{8}$$

2. What fraction is shaded?

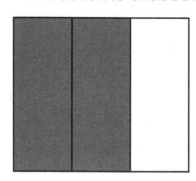

___

3. What fraction is shaded?

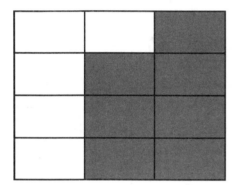

___

4. What fraction is shaded?

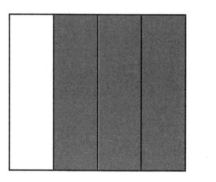

___

5. What fraction is shaded?

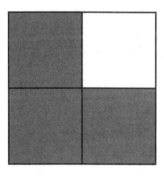

___

6. What fraction is shaded?

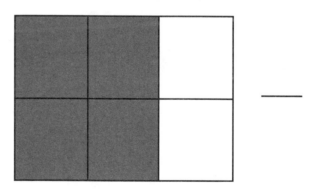

___

7. What fraction is shaded?

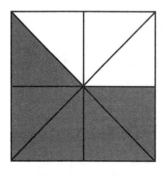

___

8. What fraction is shaded?

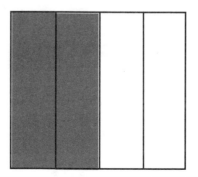

___

Name _____   Skill: Fractions

Answer the questions. The first one has been done for you.

1. What fraction is shaded?

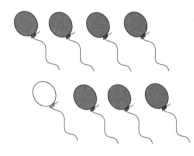
$$\frac{7}{8}$$

2. What fraction is shaded?

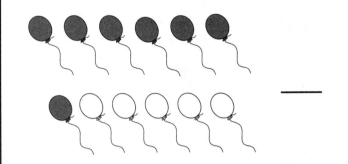
___

3. What fraction is shaded?

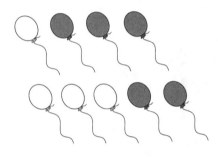
___

4. What fraction is shaded?

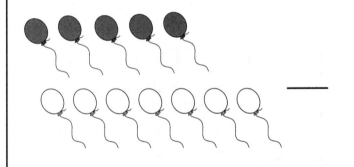
___

5. What fraction is shaded?

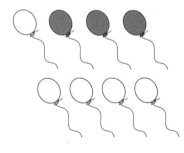
___

6. What fraction is shaded?

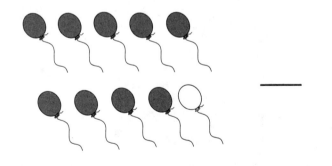
___

7. What fraction is shaded?

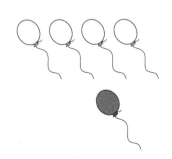
___

8. What fraction is shaded?

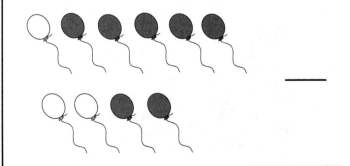
___

Name _____

Answer the questions. The first one has been done for you.

---

1. What fraction is shaded?

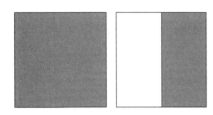 $1\frac{1}{2}$

2. What fraction is shaded?

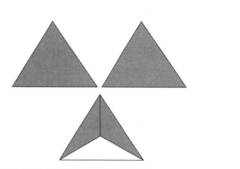   ___

---

3. What fraction is shaded?

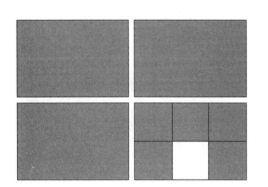   ___

4. What fraction is shaded?

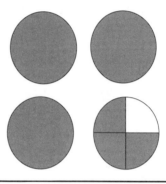   ___

---

5. What fraction is shaded?

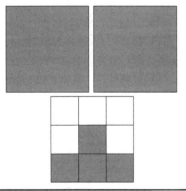   ___

6. What fraction is shaded?

   ___

---

7. What fraction is shaded?

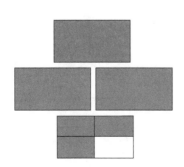   ___

8. What fraction is shaded?

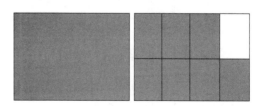   ___

Name _____ Skill: Less than, Greater than, Equal to

Compare the number sentences. Write <, >, or = in each square to make a true math statement. The first one has been done for you.

1. 5 + 8 $\boxed{<}$ 7 + 7

2. 13 − 6 $\square$ 4 + 8

3. 4 + 7 $\square$ 15 − 9

4. 6 + 6 $\square$ 9 + 2

5. 18 − 9 $\square$ 3 + 6

6. 14 − 7 $\square$ 3 + 3

7. 11 − 2 $\square$ 16 − 8

8. 2 + 8 $\square$ 16 − 6

9. 15 − 7 $\square$ 4 + 4

10. 12 − 4 $\square$ 5 + 6

11. 5 + 9 $\square$ 7 + 8

12. 7 + 5 $\square$ 4 + 8

13. 13 − 4 $\square$ 12 − 3

14. 2 + 1 $\square$ 5 − 3

15. 6 + 6 $\square$ 9 + 4

16. 7 + 9 $\square$ 8 + 8

17. 9 + 5 $\square$ 7 + 8

18. 16 − 9 $\square$ 4 + 8

19. 16 − 9 $\square$ 5 + 8

20. 6 + 4 $\square$ 14 − 8

21. 20 − 10 $\square$ 5 + 5

22. 13 − 6 $\square$ 5 + 2

23. 7 + 6 $\square$ 5 + 9

24. 4 + 5 $\square$ 16 − 7

25. 15 − 7 $\square$ 12 − 5

26. 9 + 9 $\square$ 10 + 6

27. 9 + 8 $\square$ 17 − 8

28. 15 − 9 $\square$ 4 + 1

29. 5 + 10 $\square$ 7 + 8

30. 3 + 6 $\square$ 12 − 8

Name _____ Skill: Less than, Greater than, Equal to

Compare the number sentences. Write <, >, or = in each square to make a true math statement. The first one has been done for you.

1. $11 - 6$ [<] $3 + 3$

2. $2 + 6$ [ ] $10 - 2$

3. $17 - 8$ [ ] $2 + 5$

4. $14 - 6$ [ ] $3 + 6$

5. $16 - 8$ [ ] $4 + 5$

6. $5 + 8$ [ ] $17 - 7$

7. $6 + 7$ [ ] $5 + 9$

8. $13 - 9$ [ ] $3 + 0$

9. $12 - 8$ [ ] $3 + 4$

10. $4 + 2$ [ ] $12 - 6$

11. $17 - 9$ [ ] $15 - 6$

12. $5 + 5$ [ ] $17 - 8$

13. 1×6 [ ] $6 - 0$

14. 0×4 [ ] $4 + 0$

15. $9 + 9$ [ ] 6×3

16. 5×2 [ ] $15 - 6$

17. $10 - 5$ [ ] 2×2

18. $9 - 6$ [ ] 4×2

19. 3×2 [ ] $17 - 9$

20. 1×9 [ ] $7 + 1$

21. 2×1 [ ] $8 - 5$

22. 7×3 [ ] $9 + 9$

23. 7×1 [ ] $12 - 4$

24. $8 + 8$ [ ] 8×2

25. $15 - 8$ [ ] 3×3

26. $8 - 0$ [ ] 5×0

27. 6×2 [ ] $6 + 7$

28. 7×1 [ ] $4 + 5$

29. $7 + 8$ [ ] 5×3

30. $16 - 8$ [ ] 2×4

Name _____

Read the paragraph carefully, then answer the questions. Write **NG** (not given) if there is not enough information to answer the question.

Andrea had a busy day. She got up at 7:00 in the morning. School started at 8:00 a.m. and ended at 3:30 p.m. Right after school, Andrea went to band practice for one hour. She got home half an hour later. She ate dinner at 6:00 p.m. At 7:00 p.m. she started her homework and she finished at 9:00 p.m. She went to bed at 9:30 p.m.

1. **At what time did Andrea start school?**

   _____

2. **How many hours was Andrea in school?**

   _____

3. **At what time did Andrea finish band practice?**

   _____

4. **What time was it when Andrea got home that afternoon?**

   _____

5. **How many hours did Andrea work on her homework?**

   _____

6. **At what time did she go to bed?**

   _____

7. **At what time did Andrea eat lunch?**

   _____

8. **How many hours was it from the time she got up until she went to bed?**

   _____

Name _____   Skill: Word Problems

Read the paragraph carefully, then answer the questions. Write **NG** (not given) if there is not enough information to answer the question.

Four children had a contest to see who could skate the most laps around the rink. Mr. Nerey kept the count for each child. These were the results: Charles skated 43 laps in one hour. Pam skated 16 laps and quit after 30 minutes. Jeremy skated for two hours and finished 67 laps. LeAnn skated for one and a half hours and made 86 laps.

1. Which child skated the most laps?

_____

2. Who skated for the longest time?

_____

3. How many laps did Charles and Jeremy skate altogether?

_____

4. How many laps did LeAnn and Pam skate altogether?

_____

5. How many hours did all four children skate in all?

_____

6. How many laps did all four children skate in all?

_____

7. Who counted the number of laps for each child?

_____

8. How many more laps did LeAnn skate than Charles?

_____

Read the paragraph and chart carefully, then answer the questions. Write **NG** (not given) if there is not enough information to answer the question.

Pat's friends held a frog jumping contest. Six frogs were entered. The results of the contest are listed on the chart at the right.

Spot	8 ft	3 in
Kicker	6 ft	8 in
Potsy	5 ft	2 in
Flaps	6 ft	6 in
Croaker	8 ft	4 in
Harvey	7 ft	9 in

1. **Which frog jumped the farthest?**

     _____

2. **Which frog had the shortest jump?**

     _____

3. **What is the name of the frog that came in second place?**

     _____

4. **At what time was the jumping contest held?**

     _____

5. **How much farther did Harvey jump than Potsy?**

     _____

6. **Which frogs jumped farther than 7 feet 2 inches?**

     _____

7. **How far did Flaps jump?**

     _____

8. **In which town was the frog jumping contest held?**

     _____

Name _____   Skill: Word Problems

Read the paragraph carefully, then answer the questions. Write **NG** (not given) if there is not enough information to answer the question.

    Mrs. White's third grade class held a bake sale this week. On Monday they sold 212 cupcakes. On Tuesday they sold 148 cupcakes. Wednesday was a slow day with only 43 cupcakes sold. The class did not sell cupcakes on Thursday. On Friday the group sold 271 cupcakes! They made a lot of money with cupcake sales.

1. On which day did the class not sell cupcakes?

_____

2. How many cupcakes did the class sell this week?

_____

3. On which day did they sell the most cupcakes?

_____

4. How many cupcakes were sold on Tuesday and Wednesday together?

_____

5. How many more cupcakes were sold on Friday than Monday?

_____

6. On which day did they sell the least cupcakes (<u>not</u> including Thursday)?

_____

7. How many students are in Mrs. White's third grade class?

_____

8. How many more cupcakes were sold on Monday than on Wednesday?

_____

Name _____   Skill: Word Problems

Read the paragraph carefully, then answer the questions. Write **NG** (not given) if there is not enough information to answer the question.

Dotty made a quilt. She cut lots of material into small squares and sewed them together. All of the squares were the same size. The quilt had 143 blue squares, 22 yellow squares, 119 green squares, 38 orange squares, and 74 brown squares. It took Dotty 3 months to sew all the squares together! She keeps the quilt on her bed.

1. **How long did it take Dotty to sew the quilt squares?**

   _____

2. **How many of the squares were green?**

   _____

3. **Which color did Dotty use the least?**

   _____

4. **Together, how many blue and orange squares are in the quilt?**

   _____

5. **How much did it cost to make the quilt?**

   _____

6. **How many squares did Dotty use in all?**

   _____

7. **How many more blue squares were used than brown squares?**

   _____

8. **What was the size of each square?**

   _____

Name _____   Skill: Word Problems

Read the paragraph carefully, then answer the questions. Write **NG** (not given) if there is not enough information to answer the question.

Sharon opened a lemonade stand in front of her house last summer. Sharon sold the lemonade for $1.00 per glass. Most of her customers were neighbors or family members. She made $15 in June, $22 in July, and $29 in August. Sharon used the money she made to buy a new bicycle!

1. **What kind of business did Sharon have last summer?**

_____

2. **During which three months did Sharon sell lemonade?**

_____

3. **How much did Sharon charge for a glass of lemonade?**

_____

4. **What did Sharon do with the money she made selling lemonade?**

_____

5. **During which month did Sharon make the most money?**

_____

6. **How much money did Sharon make for the month of June?**

_____

7. **How many of the neighbors bought lemonade from Sharon?**

_____

8. **How much money did Sharon make selling lemonade last summer?**

_____

Answer Key

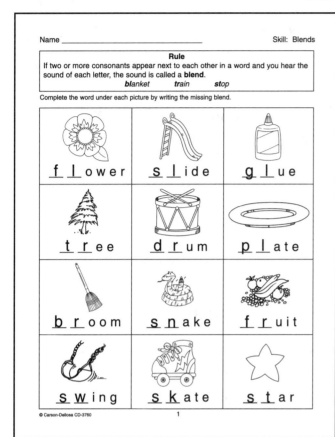

Name _____   Skill: Blends

Rule
If two or more consonants appear next to each other in a word and you hear the sound of each letter, the sound is called a **blend**.
blanket   train   stop

Complete the word under each picture by writing the missing blend.

f l ower	s l ide	g l ue
t r ee	d r um	p l ate
b r oom	s n ake	f r uit
s w ing	s k ate	s t ar

1

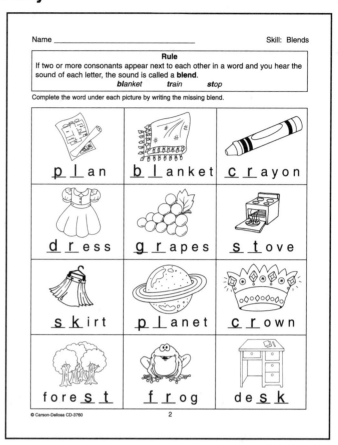

Name _____   Skill: Blends

Rule
If two or more consonants appear next to each other in a word and you hear the sound of each letter, the sound is called a **blend**.
blanket   train   stop

Complete the word under each picture by writing the missing blend.

p l an	b l anket	c r ayon
d r ess	g r apes	s t ove
s k irt	p l anet	c r own
fore s t	f r og	de s k

2

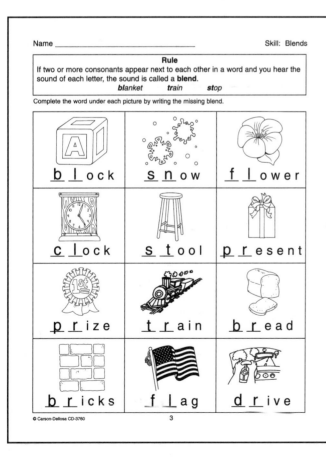

Name _____   Skill: Blends

Rule
If two or more consonants appear next to each other in a word and you hear the sound of each letter, the sound is called a **blend**.
blanket   train   stop

Complete the word under each picture by writing the missing blend.

b l ock	s n ow	f l ower
c l ock	s t ool	p r esent
p r ize	t r ain	b r ead
b r icks	f l ag	d r ive

3

Name _____   Skill: Blends

Rule
If two or more consonants appear next to each other in a word and you hear the sound of each letter, the sound is called a **blend**.
blanket   train   stop

Complete the word under each picture by writing the missing blend.

p r ice	s t ore	s l eep
s t orm	p l ane	c l ay
c l own	b r ain	ma s k
s n ail	ba s k et	p l ant

4

Answer Key

Name _____ Skill: Short Vowels

Rule

Short vowel sounds are:

a as in **pat**   e as in **pet**   i as in **pit**   o as in **pot**   u as in **put**

Read each word. Decide which sound the underlined vowel makes. Put the words with the short vowel sounds into the correct groups below. Not all the words will be used.

paint	neck	pile
pan	neat	pint
dance	jelly	rise
fancy	gentle	pickle
ham	eagle	spin
gasp	den	smile
maid	belly	sip
maple	deep	ribbon
jail	beam	rim
jacket	mend	lid
hand	smell	nip

Sounds like the "a" in *pat*	Sounds like the "e" in *pet*	Sounds like the "i" in *pit*
pan	neck	pickle
fancy	jelly	spin
ham	gentle	sip
gasp	den	ribbon
jacket	belly	rim
hand	mend	lid
dance	smell	nip

Think of a new word for each group (**short a, e, and i**).

__Answers will vary.__ _____ _____

5

Name _____ Skill: Short Vowels

Rule

Short vowel sounds are:

a as in **pat**   e as in **pet**   i as in **pit**   o as in **pot**   u as in **put**

Read each word. Decide which sound the underlined vowel makes. Put the words with the short vowel sounds into the correct groups below. Not all the words will be used.

dive	bottle	puppy
bit	block	bug
bring	drop	use
bridge	broke	junk
ice	also	truth
pie	log	bump
dig	lock	cup
hiss	poem	fuzz
thin	trot	tube
whisper	hog	dust
sight	oil	super

Sounds like the "i" in *pit*	Sounds like the "o" in *pot*	Sounds like the "u" in *put*
bit	bottle	puppy
bring	block	bug
bridge	drop	junk
dig	log	bump
hiss	lock	cup
thin	trot	fuzz
whisper	hog	dust

Think of a new word for each group (**short i, o, and u**).

__Answers will vary.__ _____ _____

6

Name _____ Skill: Short Vowels

Rule

Short vowel sounds are:

a as in **pat**   e as in **pet**   i as in **pit**   o as in **pot**   u as in **put**

Read each word. Decide which sound the underlined vowel makes. Put the words with the short vowel sounds into the correct groups below. Not all the words will be used.

time	bother	unit
clip	chop	tug
skin	common	future
dim	owe	tunnel
slide	rocket	ugly
ripe	spoil	swung
dinner	fond	true
fiddle	wove	under
mist	jolly	sudden
tip	code	just
pine	mop	rule

Sounds like the "i" in *pit*	Sounds like the "o" in *pot*	Sounds like the "u" in *put*
clip	bother	tug
skin	chop	tunnel
dim	common	ugly
dinner	rocket	swung
fiddle	fond	under
mist	jolly	sudden
tip	mop	just

Think of a new word for each group (**short i, o, and u**).

__Answers will vary.__ _____ _____

7

Name _____ Skill: Short Vowels

Rule

Short vowel sounds are:

a as in **pat**   e as in **pet**   i as in **pit**   o as in **pot**   u as in **put**

Read each word. Decide which sound the underlined vowel makes. Put the words with the short vowel sounds into the correct groups below. Not all the words will be used.

animal	even	much
began	went	pupil
ate	spell	just
made	next	cut
stand	me	January
happen	zebra	funny
table	empty	number
shape	when	human
answer	egg	hundred
back	enjoy	fruit
plant	secret	summer

Sounds like the "a" in *pat*	Sounds like the "e" in *pet*	Sounds like the "u" in *put*
animal	went	much
began	spell	just
stand	next	cut
happen	empty	funny
answer	when	number
back	egg	hundred
plant	enjoy	summer

Think of a new word for each group (**short a, e, and u**).

__Answers will vary.__ _____ _____

8

Answer Key

Worksheet (page 9)

Name _____   Skill: Long Vowels

Rule
Long vowels say their names:
a as in **lace**   e as in **easy**   i as in **ice**   o as in **open**   u as in **tuba**

Read the words in each box. Decide which sound the underlined vowel makes. Put the words with the long vowel sound into the correct group below. Not all the words will be used.

m<u>a</u>le	b<u>ea</u>n	l<u>i</u>st
<u>a</u>nswer	l<u>ea</u>f	f<u>i</u>lm
l<u>a</u>zy	str<u>ee</u>t	p<u>i</u>pe
c<u>a</u>r	<u>o</u>ver	b<u>i</u>te
tom<u>a</u>to	<u>e</u>qual	<u>i</u>dle
b<u>a</u>by	w<u>e</u>	w<u>i</u>re
f<u>a</u>ll	childr<u>e</u>n	sp<u>i</u>der
sh<u>a</u>pe	<u>ea</u>gle	w<u>i</u>de
beg<u>a</u>n	thr<u>ee</u>	l<u>i</u>fe
pl<u>a</u>y	<u>e</u>nd	gr<u>i</u>p
b<u>a</u>ke	l<u>e</u>ft	<u>i</u>ll

Sounds like the "a" in *lace*	Sounds like the "e" in *easy*	Sounds like the "i" in *ice*
male	bean	pipe
lazy	leaf	bite
tomato	street	idle
baby	equal	wire
shape	we	spider
play	eagle	wide
bake	three	life

Think of a new word for each group (**long a, e,** and **i**).

Answers will vary. _____ _____

9

Worksheet (page 10)

Name _____   Skill: Long Vowels

Rule
Long vowels say their names:
a as in **lace**   e as in **easy**   i as in **ice**   o as in **open**   u as in **tuba**

Read the words in each box. Decide which sound the underlined vowel makes. Put the words with the long vowel sound into the correct group below. Not all the words will be used.

qu<u>i</u>te	<u>o</u>ver	f<u>u</u>r
f<u>i</u>re	j<u>o</u>y	t<u>u</u>be
w<u>i</u>fe	her<u>o</u>	r<u>u</u>in
n<u>i</u>ne	st<u>o</u>p	p<u>u</u>sh
w<u>i</u>th	j<u>o</u>ke	s<u>u</u>gar
<u>i</u>nsect	b<u>o</u>wl	t<u>u</u>na
unt<u>i</u>l	t<u>o</u>ll	t<u>u</u>ne
<u>i</u>ron	p<u>o</u>le	fl<u>u</u>te
sp<u>i</u>ne	j<u>o</u>b	J<u>u</u>ne
pr<u>i</u>ce	g<u>o</u>	<u>u</u>nit
wh<u>i</u>ch	c<u>o</u>w	b<u>u</u>ll

Sounds like the "i" in *ice*	Sounds like the "o" in *open*	Sounds like the "u" in *tuba*
quite	over	tube
fire	hero	ruin
wife	joke	tuna
nine	bowl	tune
iron	toll	flute
spine	pole	June
price	go	unit

Think of a new word for each group (**long i, o,** and **u**).

Answers will vary. _____ _____

10

Worksheet (page 11)

Name _____   Skill: Long Vowels

Rule
Long vowels say their names:
a as in **lace**   e as in **easy**   i as in **ice**   o as in **open**   u as in **tuba**

Read the words in each box. Decide which sound the underlined vowel makes. Put the words with the long vowel sound into the correct group below. Not all the words will be used.

beg<u>i</u>n	b<u>o</u>ne	m<u>u</u>le
w<u>i</u>th	dr<u>o</u>p	d<u>u</u>ty
r<u>i</u>pe	<u>o</u>cean	<u>u</u>p
wh<u>i</u>te	st<u>o</u>ne	Febr<u>u</u>ary
l<u>i</u>ght	b<u>o</u>ttom	cr<u>u</u>de
m<u>i</u>nt	aw<u>o</u>ke	<u>u</u>nless
st<u>i</u>ll	fl<u>o</u>at	h<u>u</u>nt
kn<u>i</u>fe	b<u>o</u>dy	J<u>u</u>ly
w<u>i</u>ld	<u>o</u>dd	s<u>u</u>dden
h<u>i</u>ke	<u>o</u>wner	<u>u</u>seful
f<u>i</u>ne	kn<u>o</u>w	t<u>u</u>lip

Sounds like the "i" in *ice*	Sounds like the "o" in *open*	Sounds like the "u" in *tuba*
ripe	bone	mule
white	ocean	duty
light	stone	February
knife	awoke	crude
wild	float	July
hike	owner	useful
fine	know	tulip

Think of a new word for each group (**long i, o,** and **u**).

Answers will vary. _____ _____

11

Worksheet (page 12)

Name _____   Skill: Long Vowels

Rule
Long vowels say their names:
a as in **lace**   e as in **easy**   i as in **ice**   o as in **open**   u as in **tuba**

Read the words in each box. Decide which sound the underlined vowel makes. Put the words with the long vowel sound into the correct group below. Not all the words will be used.

h<u>a</u>d	r<u>ea</u>lly	r<u>u</u>de
bl<u>a</u>ck	<u>e</u>vil	r<u>e</u>gular
f<u>a</u>st	f<u>ea</u>ther	<u>u</u>ntie
w<u>ai</u>t	ch<u>ee</u>se	m<u>u</u>ch
m<u>ai</u>l	cl<u>ea</u>n	<u>i</u>nclude
ch<u>ai</u>n	r<u>ea</u>dy	<u>u</u>nite
r<u>a</u>dio	p<u>ea</u>	tr<u>u</u>th
<u>a</u>ble	t<u>e</u>n	s<u>ui</u>t
<u>a</u>pe	t<u>ee</u>th	j<u>u</u>mp
tod<u>a</u>y	p<u>ea</u>ch	<u>u</u>pset
th<u>a</u>t	t<u>e</u>ll	m<u>u</u>sic

Sounds like the "a" in *lace*	Sounds like the "e" in *easy*	Sounds like the "u" in *tuba*
wait	really	rude
mail	evil	regular
chain	cheese	include
radio	clean	unite
able	pea	truth
ape	teeth	suit
today	peach	music

Think of a new word for each group (**long a, e,** and **u**).

Answers will vary. _____ _____

12

Answer Key

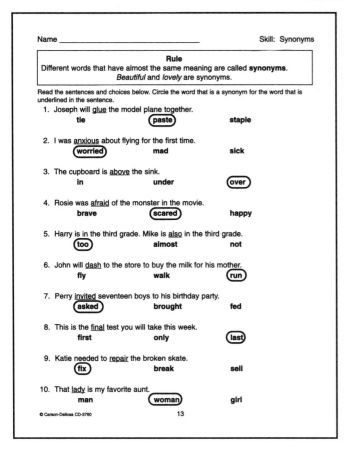

Name _____   Skill: Synonyms

Rule
Different words that have almost the same meaning are called **synonyms**.
Beautiful and *lovely* are synonyms.

Read the sentences and choices below. Circle the word that is a synonym for the word that is underlined in the sentence.

1. Joseph will glue the model plane together.
   tie   (paste)   staple

2. I was anxious about flying for the first time.
   (worried)   mad   sick

3. The cupboard is above the sink.
   in   under   (over)

4. Rosie was afraid of the monster in the movie.
   brave   (scared)   happy

5. Harry is in the third grade. Mike is also in the third grade.
   (too)   almost   not

6. John will dash to the store to buy the milk for his mother.
   fly   walk   (run)

7. Perry invited seventeen boys to his birthday party.
   (asked)   brought   fed

8. This is the final test you will take this week.
   first   only   (last)

9. Katie needed to repair the broken skate.
   (fix)   break   sell

10. That lady is my favorite aunt.
    man   (woman)   girl

© Carson-Dellosa CD-3760   13

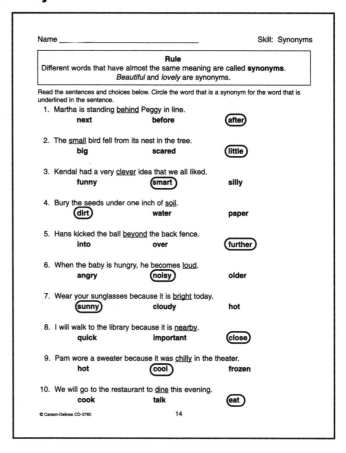

Name _____   Skill: Synonyms

Rule
Different words that have almost the same meaning are called **synonyms**.
Beautiful and *lovely* are synonyms.

Read the sentences and choices below. Circle the word that is a synonym for the word that is underlined in the sentence.

1. Martha is standing behind Peggy in line.
   next   before   (after)

2. The small bird fell from its nest in the tree.
   big   scared   (little)

3. Kendal had a very clever idea that we all liked.
   funny   (smart)   silly

4. Bury the seeds under one inch of soil.
   (dirt)   water   paper

5. Hans kicked the ball beyond the back fence.
   into   over   (further)

6. When the baby is hungry, he becomes loud.
   angry   (noisy)   older

7. Wear your sunglasses because it is bright today.
   (sunny)   cloudy   hot

8. I will walk to the library because it is nearby.
   quick   important   (close)

9. Pam wore a sweater because it was chilly in the theater.
   hot   (cool)   frozen

10. We will go to the restaurant to dine this evening.
    cook   talk   (eat)

© Carson-Dellosa CD-3760   14

Name _____   Skill: Synonyms

Rule
Different words that have almost the same meaning are called **synonyms**.
Beautiful and *lovely* are synonyms.

Read the sentences and choices below. Circle the word that is a synonym for the word that is underlined in the sentence.

1. Jeremy had an awful cold last winter.
   good   (terrible)   gentle

2. Be careful not to tear your paper!
   wrinkle   tape   (rip)

3. The boat began to sink when it hit the rock.
   (fall)   tip   float

4. The puppy was unhappy when we left the pet store.
   (sad)   scared   glad

5. The deer just sniffed the air when it heard a strange noise.
   (smelled)   tossed   stopped

6. It was difficult to say good-bye to my best friend.
   fun   easy   (hard)

7. The umbrella was still a little damp from the rain this morning.
   loose   (wet)   dry

8. My family went to a banquet in the old castle and we ate too much.
   ghost   (feast)   dance

9. Roger is the author of that story.
   reader   listen   (writer)

10. It was time to pack our bags and say farewell to our cousins.
    (good-bye)   hello   exclaim

© Carson-Dellosa CD-3760   15

Name _____   Skill: Antonyms

Rule
Words that have opposite meanings are called **antonyms**.
Before and *after* are antonyms.

Read the sentences and choices below. Circle the word that means the opposite as the word that is underlined in the sentence.

1. That lady has the keys to the car.
   (gentleman)   woman   aunt

2. Those shoes are mine.
   his   (yours)   ours

3. Jenny has a bunch of pencils in her desk.
   many   lot   (few)

4. Please help me lift this heavy box.
   small   (light)   big

5. Our class just finished reading chapter two.
   ended   (began)   enjoyed

6. Kaitlyn thinks her drawing is ugly.
   (pretty)   simple   bad

7. Cassie won the spelling bee for our school.
   entered   played   (lost)

8. Did you see that tiny mark on Dad's new car?
   small   (large)   dent

9. It is time to raise the flag.
   salute   fold   (lower)

10. Justin is the quickest runner in the group.
    (slowest)   fastest   smartest

© Carson-Dellosa CD-3760   16

Answer Key

Name _____   Skill: Antonyms

Rule
Words that have opposite meanings are called **antonyms**.
Before and *after* are antonyms.

Read the sentences and choices below. Circle the word that means the opposite as the word that is underlined in the sentence.

1. The show is just <u>beginning</u>!
   starting   wonderful   **ending**

2. Please <u>close</u> the window.
   open   clean   shut

3. Are you still <u>asleep</u>?
   sleeping   **awake**   reading

4. Put on an <u>old</u> shirt for this job.
   dirty   white   **new**

5. The pitcher threw the ball and the batter <u>missed</u> it.
   hit   threw   **caught**

6. You are acting like an <u>adult</u>.
   baby   clown   boy

7. The child was <u>smiling</u> at the puppy.
   shaking   grinning   **frowning**

8. Did you make sure that the door was <u>locked</u>?
   solid   **unlocked**   closed

9. Why is Meghan so <u>cheerful</u> today?
   happy   **gloomy**   helpful

10. The sky is so <u>clear</u> today!
    pretty   blue   **cloudy**

© Carson-Dellosa CD-3760   17

Name _____   Skill: Antonyms

Rule
Words that have opposite meanings are called **antonyms**.
Before and *after* are antonyms.

Read the sentences and choices below. Circle the word that means the opposite as the word that is underlined in the sentence.

1. It is <u>easy</u> for Jay to lift that heavy box.
   difficult   strong   silly

2. Adam arrived <u>early</u> for the party.
   late   after   before

3. I <u>never</u> like to eat pizza.
   rarely   seldom   **always**

4. You gave me the <u>wrong</u> answer to that question.
   other   **right**   simple

5. Did you <u>receive</u> a letter written for Milly?
   write   **send**   get

6. Autumn is my <u>favorite</u> season.
   loved   **disliked**   warm

7. Do not <u>drag</u> your book bag down the hall!
   pull   **push**   carry

8. Susan was really <u>calm</u> during the storm.
   excited   quiet   still

9. The girls were <u>noisy</u> as they entered the school.
   quiet   running   loud

10. Giving you a ride was the <u>least</u> I could do.
    only   nice   **most**

© Carson-Dellosa CD-3760   18

Name _____   Skill: Homophones

Rule
Words that are pronounced the same way but have different meanings and spellings are called **homophones**.
Flower and *flour* are homophones.

Read the sentences and choices below. For each sentence, write the correct homophone in the blank.

1. An _____ant_____ crawled across the sidewalk.
   ant   aunt

2. There are _____eight_____ colors in my rainbow.
   ate   eight

3. _____I_____ am nine years old.
   I   eye

4. Can you _____add_____ big numbers?
   ad   add

5. That _____bee_____ is building a hive.
   be   bee

6. Where did the dog _____bury_____ his bone?
   berry   bury

7. The wind _____blew_____ hard last night!
   blew   blue

8. I used the _____brakes_____ to stop my bike.
   brakes   breaks

9. How much ice cream did you _____buy_____?
   buy   by   bye

10. Rachel _____sent_____ a letter to her friend.
    cent   scent   sent

© Carson-Dellosa CD-3760   19

Name _____   Skill: Homophones

Rule
Words that are pronounced the same way but have different meanings and spellings are called **homophones**.
Flower and *flour* are homophones.

Read the sentences and choices below. For each sentence, write the correct homophone in the blank.

1. That _____plane_____ is flying awfully low!
   plain   plane

2. What game did you _____choose_____ to play?
   choose   chews

3. Pick up those _____clothes_____ and hang them up!
   close   clothes

4. Winston sailed his toy boat down the _____creek_____.
   creak   creek

5. Mom _____dyed_____ my shirt blue.
   died   dyed

6. That rabbit's _____fur_____ makes me sneeze!
   fir   fur

7. A bluebird _____flew_____ to the maple tree.
   flew   flu

8. Use two cups of _____flour_____ to make this cake.
   flour   flower

9. Kyle _____knew_____ everything on the test.
   new   knew   gnu

10. Would you like milk _____or_____ soda to drink?
    oar   or   ore

© Carson-Dellosa CD-3760   20

Answer Key

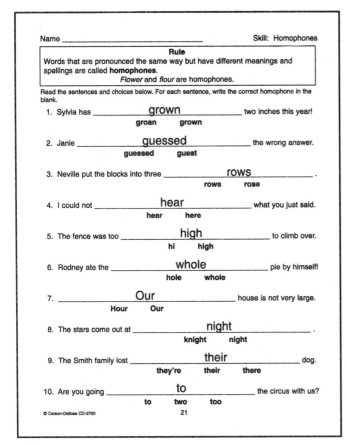

Name _____ Skill: Homophones

Rule
Words that are pronounced the same way but have different meanings and spellings are called **homophones**.
Flower and *flour* are homophones.

Read the sentences and choices below. For each sentence, write the correct homophone in the blank.

1. Sylvia has _____**grown**_____ two inches this year!
   groan   grown

2. Janie _____**guessed**_____ the wrong answer.
   guessed   guest

3. Neville put the blocks into three _____**rows**_____ .
   rows   rose

4. I could not _____**hear**_____ what you just said.
   hear   here

5. The fence was too _____**high**_____ to climb over.
   hi   high

6. Rodney ate the _____**whole**_____ pie by himself!
   hole   whole

7. _____**Our**_____ house is not very large.
   Hour   Our

8. The stars come out at _____**night**_____ .
   knight   night

9. The Smith family lost _____**their**_____ dog.
   they're   their   there

10. Are you going _____**to**_____ the circus with us?
    to   two   too

© Carson-Dellosa CD-3760   21

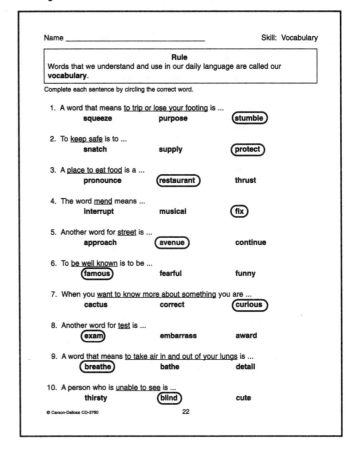

Name _____ Skill: Vocabulary

Rule
Words that we understand and use in our daily language are called our **vocabulary**.

Complete each sentence by circling the correct word.

1. A word that means <u>to trip or lose your footing</u> is ...
   squeeze   purpose   (stumble)

2. To <u>keep safe</u> is to ...
   snatch   supply   (protect)

3. A <u>place to eat food</u> is a ...
   pronounce   (restaurant)   thrust

4. The word <u>mend</u> means ...
   interrupt   musical   (fix)

5. Another word for <u>street</u> is ...
   approach   (avenue)   continue

6. To <u>be well known</u> is to be ...
   (famous)   fearful   funny

7. When you <u>want to know more about something</u> you are ...
   cactus   correct   (curious)

8. Another word for <u>test</u> is ...
   (exam)   embarrass   award

9. A word that means <u>to take air in and out of your lungs</u> is ...
   (breathe)   bathe   detail

10. A person who is <u>unable to see</u> is ...
    thirsty   (blind)   cute

© Carson-Dellosa CD-3760   22

Name _____ Skill: Vocabulary

Rule
Words that we understand and use in our daily language are called our **vocabulary**.

Complete each sentence by circling the correct word.

1. A word <u>that means the day before today</u> is ...
   (yesterday)   tomorrow   behold

2. To <u>disappear</u> is to ...
   watch   (vanish)   trumpet

3. A <u>group of twelve</u> is a ...
   (dozen)   tortoise   trickle

4. A word that means <u>to get ready</u> is ...
   prevent   stew   (prepare)

5. Another word for <u>rare</u> is ...
   position   (unusual)   startle

6. To <u>make something pointed</u> is to ...
   (sharpen)   silence   rattle

7. When you <u>talk something over with another person</u> you ...
   (discuss)   dusk   bounce

8. Another word for <u>real</u> is ...
   admire   (actual)   account

9. A <u>short coat</u> is a ...
   guitar   helmet   (jacket)

10. A person who <u>flies a plane</u> is a ...
    borrow   dentist   (pilot)

© Carson-Dellosa CD-3760   23

Name _____ Skill: Vocabulary

Rule
Words that we understand and use in our daily language are called our **vocabulary**.

Complete each sentence by circling the correct word.

1. A word that means <u>far away</u> is ...
   carve   dare   (distant)

2. To <u>address with kind wishes</u> is to ...
   fig   grind   (greet)

3. A <u>grown-up person</u> is an ...
   (adult)   alphabet   audience

4. Another word for <u>trap</u> is ...
   cliff   (capture)   fellow

5. The word <u>eager</u> means ...
   carriage   disturb   (anxious)

6. To <u>decide on something</u> is to ...
   (choose)   calm   bandage

7. When <u>you make something new</u> you ...
   (create)   double   bore

8. Another word for <u>afraid</u> is ...
   familiar   farewell   (fearful)

9. A word that means <u>total or all</u> is ...
   dawn   (entire)   faint

10. A person who <u>cuts meat</u> is a ...
    designer   (butcher)   carpenter

© Carson-Dellosa CD-3760   24

Answer Key

Name _____   Skill: Classification

Rule
Words that have something in common can be sorted into groups called **categories.**

| pencil (school supply) | tent (camping supply) |
| paper (school supply) | sleeping bag (camping supply) |

All of these words belong to the same big category. Name how they are alike in the "Main Heading." Sort the words into two groups, or subcategories. Put the title of each group on the line "Subheading."

orange	onion	raspberry	spinach
carrot	apple	radish	cherry
celery	beet	lettuce	grape
plum	banana	lemon	squash
blueberry	potato	peach	peas

Main Heading:	Food	
Subheading: **fruits**	Subheading: **vegetables**	
orange	carrot
plum	celery
blueberry	onion
apple	beet
banana	potato
raspberry	radish
lemon	lettuce
peach	spinach
cherry	squash
grape	pea

25

Name _____   Skill: Classification

Rule
Words that have something in common can be sorted into groups called **categories.**

| pencil (school supply) | tent (camping supply) |
| paper (school supply) | sleeping bag (camping supply) |

All of these words belong to the same big category. Name how they are alike in the "Main Heading." Sort the words into two groups, or subcategories. Put the title of each group on the line "Subheading."

Ellen	Mark	Nancy	Jane
George	Joe	Paul	Bob
Cindy	Mary	Anne	Marsha
David	Peter	Greg	Mike
Diana	Larry	Peggy	Laura

Main Heading:	Names	
Subheading: **boys' names**	Subheading: **girls' names**	
George	Ellen
David	Cindy
Mark	Diana
Joe	Mary
Peter	Nancy
Larry	Anne
Paul	Peggy
Greg	Jane
Bob	Marsha
Mike	Laura

26

Name _____   Skill: Classification

Rule
Words that have something in common can be sorted into groups called **categories.**

| pencil (school supply) | tent (camping supply) |
| paper (school supply) | sleeping bag (camping supply) |

All of these words belong to the same big category. Name how they are alike in the "Main Heading." Sort the words into two groups, or subcategories. Put the title of each group on the line "Subheading."

store	King Library	Yellowstone Park	hospital
park	D.C. High School	bridge	Las Vegas
Elm Avenue	Main Street Mall	building	river
school	street	Golden Gate Bridge	library
city	Care Hospital	Mississippi River	Super Dome

Main Heading:	Nouns	
Subheading: **proper nouns**	Subheading: **common nouns**	
Elm Avenue	store
King Library	park
D.C. High School	school
Main Street Mall	city
Care Hospital	street
Yellowstone Park	bridge
Golden Gate Bridge	building
Mississippi River	hospital
Las Vegas	river
Super Dome	library

27

Name _____   Skill: Context Clues

Rule
When you come to a word you don't know, use the **context clues** (the meaning of the rest of the sentence or paragraph) to help you understand its meaning.

Use the context clues to figure out the meaning of each underlined word below. Circle the correct meaning.

1. The oil made the street slick, and the car tires slid on it.
   (slippery)   sticky   sweet

2. Brian was filled with grief when his best friend moved away.
   happiness   hate   (sadness)

3. Kelsey put the money into a pouch she kept on her belt.
   (bag)   dress   bottle

4. We don't have much time, so please give a brief speech.
   nasty   slow   (short)

5. I plunged right into the pool, but my sister took her time getting wet.
   waded   (jumped)   pulled

6. We will release the bird from the cage when its broken wing is better.
   hide   capture   (set free)

7. We baked a batch of cookies for the bake sale.
   one   (group)   kind

8. This antique chair was used by a king.
   pretty   (very old)   new

9. The directions tell us to combine the eggs and flour to make the cake.
   separate   sell   (mix)

10. Use caution when trying to cross a busy street.
    (safety)   rudeness   cars

28

Answer Key

Name _____ Skill: Context Clues

Rule
When you come to a word you don't know, use the **context clues** (the meaning of the rest of the sentence or paragraph) to help you understand its meaning.

Use the context clues to figure out the meaning of each underlined word below. Circle the correct meaning.

1. My face turned crimson when I blushed.
   green (red) pale

2. The gravel in the driveway crunched under the tires of the car.
   grass (small stones) cement

3. I did not hesitate to help when the old man fell down the steps.
   (wait) jump move

4. We put the books in a crate before we shipped them to Mexico.
   wastebasket (wooden box) bag

5. I detest that television show!
   enjoy love (dislike)

6. The umbrella wouldn't open, so it was useless.
   (not helpful) nice broken

7. The beef was tough to chew.
   soft tasty (hard)

8. The room began to sway when the earthquake hit.
   (rock) light up sing

9. Don't just tear the paper. Shred it so no one can read it.
   (make tiny pieces) tape together throw away

10. Shelly was so timid, she hid when the children came over to play.
    old (shy) pretty

© Carson-Dellosa CD-3760   29

Name _____ Skill: Context Clues

Rule
When you come to a word you don't know, use the **context clues** (the meaning of the rest of the sentence or paragraph) to help you understand its meaning.

Use the context clues to figure out the meaning of each underlined word below. Circle the correct meaning.

1. My legs tremble when I am scared.
   (shake) faint strong

2. The bakery had various types of cookies from which we could choose.
   one (different) none

3. The chocolate milk shake was a tasty treat!
   (good) awful ugly

4. We squinted our eyes as we walked outside into the brilliant light.
   dull (bright) new

5. Trevor began to argue with his sister over who would get the new game.
   tease talk (fight)

6. Trenice walked down the aisle of the theater, looking for a good seat.
   (pathway) screen building

7. The fuzzy peach flesh felt soft as a baby mouse!
   feet (skin) cage

8. Ten dollars seems expensive for a kite.
   (costly) cheap soft

9. Larry deserves a reward for that brave deed.
   (earns) gives decides

10. I cannot recall how many children were at the party last week.
    tell speak (remember)

© Carson-Dellosa CD-3760   30

Name _____ Skill: Context Clues

Rule
When you come to a word you don't know, use the **context clues** (the meaning of the rest of the sentence or paragraph) to help you understand its meaning.

Use the context clues to figure out the meaning of each underlined word below. Circle the correct meaning.

1. This route to the grocery store takes me past your house.
   travel (way) cart

2. We saw clowns and rode the roller coaster at the carnival.
   camp parade (fair)

3. Mr. Spade will conduct the orchestra next week.
   feed (lead) move

4. The young boy began to wail when he could not find his mother.
   jump (cry) bang

5. I intend to find out who took my watch!
   (plan) hate will not

6. We must divide this box of apples into two groups.
   (separate) crust lift

7. Jonas felt cozy under the warm blankets.
   cold frightened (snug)

8. The fresh paint looked glossy in the sun.
   (shiny) dull blue

9. The hoot of the owl sounded eerie in the darkness.
   stubborn (strange) happy

10. The glass vase shattered when it hit the floor.
    dented (broke) rang out

© Carson-Dellosa CD-3760   31

Name _____ Skill: Fiction Comprehension

Rule
Understanding what happens in a story is called **comprehension**.

Read the story, then answer the questions about it.

Greg and Calvin hopped off the subway at the stadium. Today was the biggest game of the baseball season, but neither boy had a ticket. They seemed to be in luck. No one was standing in line for tickets! As they reached the ticket booth, they saw why. A large sign said, "SOLD OUT!" Greg and Calvin could hear the crowd roar as the game began. They were very disappointed. The boys began to walk across the parking lot, back to the subway. The crowd behind them roared again as a ball flew over the wall and landed near their feet. Maybe this game would be fun after all!

1. **A good title for this story would be:**
   a. A Ride on the Subway
   (b) Baseball in the Parking Lot
   c. The Roar of the Crowd

2. **What were the boys hoping to buy?** The boys were hoping to buy tickets to a baseball game.

3. **What is a word that means "a sports park or arena"?**
   a. roared
   b. disappointed
   (c) stadium

4. **Why couldn't the boys get in to see the game?** The boys couldn't get in to see the game because it was sold out.

5. **What happened that made the boys happy about the game?** A ball landed near their feet.

6. **What would you do if you were the boys?** Answers will vary.

© Carson-Dellosa CD-3760   32

Answer Key

Name _____ Skill: Fiction Comprehension

Rule
Understanding what happens in a story is called **comprehension**.

Read the story, then answer the questions about it.

Nan blushed as the teacher called her name. It was her turn to stand in front of the class and give her book report. Nan slowly pulled out her paper and stood up. Her feet felt heavy as she walked to the front of the room. She could feel the eyes of every person in the class watching her, waiting for her to begin. Nan did not even look at the class as she began to read. The first word out of her mouth sounded just like a frog croaking! Nan turned red and cleared her throat. She wished she could just disappear. Writing reports was fun, but giving them was difficult.

1. **A good title for this story would be:**
   (a.) The Book Report
   b. The Class Laughs
   c. The Frogs are Croaking
2. **Why does Nan walk to the front of the room?** She had to give a book report.
3. **What is a word that means "turned red"?**
   a. disappear
   b. heavy
   (c.) blushed
4. **How does Nan feel about giving reports to the class?** Nan felt nervous.
5. **Name two things in the story that show us how Nan is feeling.** She turned deep red. She cleared her throat.
6. **What could Nan do to make reporting easier?** Answers will vary.

Name _____ Skill: Fiction Comprehension

Rule
Understanding what happens in a story is called **comprehension**.

Read the story, then answer the questions about it.

Luke groaned as he tried to sit up in bed. Yesterday he had been riding his bike when he fell and broke his leg. The doctor had set the bone and put on a cast. He had spent the night in the hospital, but now he was back at home. His leg was throbbing and the cast felt like it weighed a ton. Worst of all, Luke had an itch on his knee, but he couldn't reach it through the cast. Luke began to feel very sorry for himself. He would be stuck in this cast for the rest of summer vacation. What horrible luck! Even if his friends wanted to come see him, Luke wouldn't be able to do much with them.

1. **A good title for this story would be:**
   (a.) A Broken Leg
   b. Luke is Sick
   c. The Itchy Knee
2. **How did Luke break his leg?** Luke broke his leg when he fell off his bike.
3. **What is a word that means "very bad"?**
   (a.) horrible
   b. throbbing
   c. hospital
4. **How is Luke feeling in this story? Why?** He feels sorry for himself because he will have a cast on all summer.
5. **Name two things that are bad about the cast.** The cast weighs a lot. He couldn't scratch his leg.
6. **What would you do to cheer Luke?** Answers will vary.

Name _____ Skill: Fiction Comprehension

Rule
Understanding what happens in a story is called **comprehension**.

Read the story, then answer the questions about it.

Jackie sat quietly in the tree house. She lowered her head so she could not see over the wall and began to listen to the sounds of her neighborhood. Jackie could tell that her neighbor, Mrs. Sanders, had her kitchen window open because she could hear the sound of dishes being washed in the sink. She could hear a dog barking farther down the block. Jackie closed her eyes and listened harder. She could hear the tinkle of wind chimes and leaves rustling in the gentle breeze. She heard the buzz of a mosquito as it flitted around her head, looking for a place where it might land.

1. **A good title for this story would be:**
   a. What Jackie Saw
   (b.) The Sounds of the Neighborhood
   c. The Tree House
2. **Where was Jackie sitting?** Jackie was sitting in her tree house.
3. **What is a word that means "a light, ringing sound"?**
   a. gentle
   b. flitted
   (c.) tinkle
4. **What was Mrs. Sanders doing?** Mrs. Sanders was washing dishes.
5. **Why do you think Jackie "closed her eyes" to listen harder?** Answers will vary.
6. **What do you think Jackie's mood is? Explain.** Answers will vary.

Name _____ Skill: Fiction Comprehension

Rule
Understanding what happens in a story is called **comprehension**.

Read the story, then answer the questions about it.

Hetty sat by herself at the corner of the playground. She felt like crying, but didn't want the other kids to see her. What a horrible morning. Melody had brought a beautiful ring to school and all the girls really liked it. Melody left it on her desk when she went to the bathroom and it was gone when she returned. Hetty sat next to Melody, and now all the girls were saying that she had stolen the ring. How could Melody think that Hetty had taken it? They were best friends and Hetty would never do something like that. The other girls were whispering and looking at Hetty now. How could she prove that she was innocent?

1. **A good title for this story would be:**
   a. Hetty is a Thief
   b. A Day at School
   (c.) The Missing Ring
2. **What had happened in class that morning?** Melody's ring was missing. Everyone was blaming Hetty.
3. **What is a word that means "came back"?**
   (a.) returned
   b. stolen
   c. playground
4. **Why did Melody think that Hetty may have taken the ring?** Hetty sat next to Melody.
5. **What word might describe how Hetty is feeling? Explain why.** Answers will vary (sad, unhappy, hurt).
6. **What would you do if you were Hetty?** Answers will vary.

Answer Key

Name _____ Skill: Nonfiction Comprehension

Rule
Understanding what happens in a story is called **comprehension**.

Read the story, then answer the questions about it.

A community is a group of people that live in the same area. Many people live and work in your community. Early people used to live in small family groups. They produced everything from the food they ate to the clothes they wore. As people became more civilized, they began to depend on each other for their special skills. One family would make shoes and another grew crops. Families began to settle closer together and trade for the things they needed. As more families grouped together, communities were formed.

1. **A good title for this story would be:**
   a. Our Family Makes Shoes
   b. How Families Live
   c. Why We Live in Communities
2. **What groups did people live in during the early years?** People
lived in small family groups.
3. **Which word means "a group of people living and working together"?**
   a. civilized
   b. community
   c. formed
4. **Name two things from the story that people do in communities.**
People live and work together in communities.
5. **Why do you think being civilized made people need each other more?**
Answers will vary.

6. **Name something you think you would like to do in a community. Why?**
Answers will vary.

© Carson-Dellosa CD-3760   37

Name _____ Skill: Nonfiction Comprehension

Rule
Understanding what happens in a story is called **comprehension**.

Read the story, then answer the questions about it.

Language is the most important thing ever invented. Language allows us to communicate, or share information, with each other. It is what lets us share thoughts and ideas and explain how we feel or what we need. No matter what language you speak, you are communicating through words. Words are used when we talk on the phone, write a letter or telegram, listen to the radio, read a book, or watch a movie. Even people who can't hear use language to communicate. They speak with hand signals. What a lonely place this world would be without language!

1. **A good title for this story would be:**
   a. Some People Use Sign Language
   b. Language Is Important
   c. How to Write a Telegram
2. **According to this story, what is the most important invention of all?**
Language is the most important invention.

3. **What is a word that means "to share information"?**
   a. language
   b. communicate
   c. signal
4. **How do people who can't hear use language?** People who
cannot hear use hand signals.

5. **Name two ways of communicating that are not listed in the story:**
Answers will vary.

6. **What was the last communication you had with another person?**
Answers will vary.

© Carson-Dellosa CD-3760   38

Name _____ Skill: Nonfiction Comprehension

Rule
Understanding what happens in a story is called **comprehension**.

Read the story, then answer the questions about it.

From where does the milk you drink come? If your answer is, "a cow," you are probably right. However, did you know that not everyone drinks cow's milk? Children in Lapland drink milk from reindeer. In India, milk often comes from the water buffalo. Arab children like the rich, thick milk that comes from camels, and Greek children think goat's milk is the best. If you are in Tibet, you may drink a glass of yak milk. Some babies have an allergy to animal milk, and it makes them sick. They might have a bottle of milk that doesn't come from any animal at all. It is soy milk made from soybeans!

1. **A good title for this story would be:**
   a. Different Kinds of Milk
   b. Some Babies Drink Soy Milk
   c. Milk Comes from Cows
2. **What kind of milk would a Greek child drink?** A Greek child
would drink goat's milk.

3. **What is a word that means "something that causes a rash or illness"?**
   a. a reindeer
   b. soybeans
   c. an allergy
4. **Name three animals in the story that give milk.** Cow, reindeer,
water buffalo, camel, goat, and yak all give milk.

5. **Why do some babies drink soy milk?** Some babies drink soy
milk because they are allergic to animal milk.

6. **What type of milk would you not like to try? Why?**
Answers will vary.

© Carson-Dellosa CD-3760   39

Name _____ Skill: Nonfiction Comprehension

Rule
Understanding what happens in a story is called **comprehension**.

Read the story, then answer the questions about it.

Your first name is probably the first gift you ever received from your family. You may be named after a favorite uncle or aunt. Your name may be a reminder of something that happened around the time you were born. Your name may simply be one that your parents liked. Whatever your name, it might be one that you can find anywhere in the world. The English name *John* is *Juan* in Spanish, *Johann* in German, *Ivan* in Russian, and *Sean* in Irish. The Irish *Moira*, Italian *Maria*, and French *Marie* are all the same as the English name *Mary*. Do you know what your name is in another country?

1. **A good title for this story would be:**
   a. John and Mary around the World
   b. Named after Grandfather
   c. What's in a Name?
2. **What is the English name for the French *Marie*?** *Mary* is the
English name for *Marie*.
3. **What is a word that means "a thing to help you remember"?**
   a. Italian
   b. country
   c. reminder
4. **What is the name for *John* in Russian? In Spanish?** In Russian,
John is *Ivan*. In Spanish, it is *Juan*.

5. **Why do you think people have first names?** Answers will vary.

6. **Why did your family give you your first name?** Answers will vary.

© Carson-Dellosa CD-3760   40

Answer Key

Name _____ Skill: Nonfiction Comprehension

Rule
Understanding what happens in a story is called **comprehension**.

Read the story, then answer the questions about it.

How many times have teachers told you that you weren't paying attention? Does it happen often? There are many things that affect our attention. If you haven't had enough sleep, it is hard to focus on your studies. Some children are easily distracted, or have their thoughts drawn away, by something else that is happening in the classroom. Sometimes the buzz of the lights or the grinding pencil sharpener can cause you to drift away from what the teacher is saying. You *are* paying attention, but not to the most important things. If you are easily distracted, you might try sitting closer to the front of the room near the teacher.

1. A good title for this story would be:
   a. Teachers are Mean
   b. Lights that Buzz
   (c.) Paying Attention
2. What are two things named in the story that might be distracting?_____

   buzzing lights, grinding pencil sharpeners
3. What is a word that means "to draw away attention"?
   a. focus
   (b.) distract
   c. grinding
4. Why might the teacher think a student is not paying attention?_____

   Answers will vary.
5. What can you do to help yourself pay better attention?_____

   Answers will vary.
6. What things in your classroom are distracting? Explain._____

   Answers will vary.

© Carson-Dellosa CD-3760   41

Name _____ Skill: Letter Comprehension

Rule
Letters are messages that we write to other people or organizations.

Read the letter below, then answer the questions about it.

June 15

Dear Max,

Next week my family is leaving for our vacation. We are going to Mount Rushmore to see the Presidents' faces on the mountain. We will be gone for two weeks.

Would you do me a favor? My parents won't let me take Muffin with us on the trip. She can stay in her cage, but she needs to be fed and watered every day. She also needs to have her coat and long ears brushed once a week. If you will take care of her for me, I'd be very grateful. I even promise to bring you a nice gift from our travels. Please let me know if you can take care of Muffin. Thanks a lot.

Your friend,
Marvin

1. What does Marvin ask Max to do? Marvin asks Max to take

   care of his pet while he is on vacation.
2. What is a word that means "thankful"?
   a. vacation
   b. promise
   (c.) grateful
3. Where is Marvin's family going? Marvin's family is going

   to Mount Rushmore.
4. What must Max do to take care of Muffin? Max will need to feed,

   water, and brush Muffin each day.
5. What kind of animal do you think Muffin is? Explain why._____

   Answers will vary.

© Carson-Dellosa CD-3760   42

Name _____ Skill: Letter Comprehension

Rule
Letters are messages that we write to other people or organizations.

Read the letter below, then answer the questions about it.

February 21

Dear Mr. Piper,

Our Boy Scout troop would like to thank you for coming to our meeting last week. We enjoyed hearing about your experiences as a sailor. It was exciting to hear your story about that big storm at sea and how it pushed your ship around. We all thought the story about the new cook and the food he made was very funny! Best of all, we enjoyed learning how to tie the knots you showed us. Our Scout Master had us practice the knots all week and will give us a test on them this Saturday.

Thank you so much for sharing your stories and knowledge with us. Please come back and visit us again!

Sincerely,
Troop 709

1. Why did Troop 709 write this letter to Mr. Piper? They wanted to

   thank him for coming to their meeting.
2. What is a word that means "to learn by doing something over and over"?
   a. knots
   (b.) practice
   c. sharing
3. Which story of Mr. Piper's was funny? The story about the new

   cook and the food he made was funny.
4. On which information will the troop have a test next Saturday? The

   troop will be tested on making knots.
5. What would you like to ask a sailor? Explain._____

   Answers will vary.

© Carson-Dellosa CD-3760   43

Name _____ Skill: Letter Comprehension

Rule
Letters are messages that we write to other people or organizations.

Read the letter below, then answer the questions about it.

March 9

Dear Kim Lei,

I told my teacher about Tet, your country's New Year celebration. She found information about your holiday and taught my whole class about it! We had a Tet party, too! We read about the dance with the dragon that chases away evil spirits. Everyone helped make a huge dragon mask, and we did the dragon dance through the halls. We also gave each other red envelopes filled with nice sayings and a little money, just as you do in your country. Our Tet celebration was not as important as yours, but we all enjoyed it and learned a lot more about your country!

Your pen pal,
Susan

1. What is Susan telling Kim Lei in this letter? Susan is telling

   Kim Lei about the Tet celebration in her class.
2. What is a word that means "an occasion or event being observed"?
   (a.) celebration
   b. spirits
   c. country
3. What is the purpose of the dragon dance? The dragon dance

   chases away the evil spirits.
4. What did the children put into the red envelopes? They put nice

   sayings and money in the envelopes.
5. Is it good to learn about customs from other countries? Why or why not?

   Answers will vary.

© Carson-Dellosa CD-3760   44

Answer Key

Name _____   Skill: Nouns

Rule
A **noun** is a word that names a person, place, or thing. The underlined words are nouns.
The girl rode to school on the bus.

Underline every noun in each sentence.

1. An <u>acorn</u> will grow into an oak <u>tree</u>.

2. When a <u>child</u> grows up, she becomes an <u>adult</u>.

3. I need one more <u>dime</u> to pay for this <u>pen</u>.

4. The <u>boat</u> pulled up to the <u>dock</u>.

5. You need to use your <u>brain</u> to learn!

6. <u>Brad</u> is a really nice <u>boy</u>.

7. It is so hot, I think I will have a cold <u>glass</u> of <u>lemonade</u>.

8. The <u>grass</u> is getting long, so it is <u>time</u> to mow the <u>lawn</u>.

9. The <u>soldier</u> went to boot <u>camp</u> for six <u>weeks</u>.

10. Would you like to be my <u>partner</u> for the field <u>trip</u>?

11. <u>Beth</u> and <u>Amy</u> will work together on the <u>report</u>.

12. <u>Brittney</u> wore a <u>hat</u> and <u>mittens</u> today.

13. The large <u>butterfly</u> fluttered near the <u>flowers</u> in the <u>garden</u>.

14. My <u>feet</u> were cold after playing in the <u>snow</u>.

© Carson-Dellosa CD-3760   45

Name _____   Skill: Nouns

Rule
A **noun** is a word that names a person, place, or thing. The underlined words are nouns.
The girl rode to school on the bus.

Underline every noun in each sentence.

1. That book <u>report</u> is due <u>Monday</u>.

2. The <u>headlights</u> on that <u>car</u> are very bright!

3. We caught a <u>lizard</u> in the <u>desert</u>.

4. It got cold enough to leave a little <u>frost</u> on the <u>grass</u> last <u>night</u>.

5. The <u>future</u> is ahead of us!

6. That <u>customer</u> bought <u>groceries</u> <u>today</u>.

7. A pretty <u>bluebird</u> was singing in the <u>tree</u>.

8. The <u>carpenter</u> built the <u>cupboards</u> for <u>Mom</u>.

9. The <u>bird</u> left its <u>footprints</u> under the <u>window</u>!

10. The <u>chickens</u> were clucking in the <u>barnyard</u>.

11. <u>Brian</u> counted the <u>ants</u> as they marched across the <u>sidewalk</u>.

12. Do not ride a <u>bike</u> on busy <u>streets</u>!

13. <u>Jason</u> turned on the <u>lights</u> because the <u>room</u> was dark.

14. The <u>baby</u> had three stuffed <u>animals</u> in her <u>crib</u>.

© Carson-Dellosa CD-3760   46

Name _____   Skill: Nouns

Rule
A **noun** is a word that names a person, place, or thing. The underlined words are nouns.
The girl rode to school on the bus.

Underline every noun in each sentence.

1. <u>Johnny</u> is a <u>member</u> of the drama <u>club</u>.

2. The mail <u>carrier</u> left a <u>package</u> at the <u>door</u>.

3. The <u>dolphin</u> waved his <u>flipper</u> as he swam away.

4. The <u>child</u> wore <u>moccasins</u> on her <u>feet</u>.

5. <u>Jacob</u> filled the <u>tank</u> with <u>gas</u> this <u>morning</u>.

6. The <u>cowboys</u> rode into the <u>canyon</u>.

7. My favorite <u>fruit</u> is the <u>banana</u>.

8. We roasted <u>marshmallows</u> over the <u>campfire</u>.

9. My <u>aunt's</u> <u>daughter</u> is my <u>cousin</u>.

10. <u>Mrs. Greene</u> and her <u>husband</u> took a <u>trip</u>.

11. The <u>house</u> on the <u>corner</u> has a big <u>porch</u>.

12. The <u>deer</u> ran into the <u>forest</u> when it heard the <u>car</u> coming.

13. The <u>artist</u> paints <u>pictures</u> of <u>birds</u>.

14. <u>Nathan</u> could not find his <u>belt</u>.

© Carson-Dellosa CD-3760   47

Name _____   Skill: Nouns

Rule
A **noun** is a word that names a person, place, or thing. The underlined words are nouns.
The girl rode to school on the bus.

Underline every noun in each sentence.

1. I keep sixteen <u>goldfish</u> in my <u>pond</u>.

2. Put on a <u>sweater</u> because it is chilly <u>today</u>!

3. <u>Charlene</u> wore a red <u>ribbon</u> in her <u>hair</u>.

4. I like to look at old <u>photographs</u> of <u>people</u>.

5. The <u>children</u> made <u>puppets</u> to put on a <u>show</u> at <u>school</u>.

6. The <u>farmer</u> cut the <u>wheat</u> in his <u>field</u>.

7. <u>Jenny</u> wrote the <u>letter</u> on the <u>computer</u>.

8. The <u>birds</u> sat on the <u>ledge</u> of the tall <u>building</u>.

9. The <u>hunter</u> had a log <u>cabin</u> deep in the <u>woods</u>.

10. The <u>knight</u> wore heavy <u>armor</u> into <u>battle</u>.

11. Three <u>boys</u> will sing this <u>song</u> at the <u>concert</u>.

12. <u>Benjamin</u> wore old <u>clothes</u> when he painted the <u>house</u>.

13. The <u>box</u> of <u>candy</u> costs four <u>dollars</u>.

14. <u>Marvin</u> had a <u>sandwich</u> and <u>carrots</u> for <u>lunch</u>.

© Carson-Dellosa CD-3760   48

© Carson-Dellosa CD-3760   109

Answer Key

Name _____ Skill: Verbs

Rule
A **verb** is a word that shows action. The underlined words are verbs.
The boy ran to the field to play soccer.

Underline every verb in each sentence.

1. I <u>included</u> a drink in your lunchbox.

2. This magician will <u>amaze</u> you with his tricks!

3. That scientist <u>discovered</u> and <u>named</u> a new star.

4. We <u>were</u> excited about the trip.

5. Those rocks were <u>formed</u> by the volcano.

6. Stacy <u>mumbled</u> so no one could <u>hear</u> her.

7. The ball was <u>thrown</u> into the bushes.

8. <u>Stir</u> the soup while I <u>get</u> the bowls.

9. Please <u>repeat</u> the directions.

10. The firefighters will <u>rescue</u> the kitten from the tree.

11. We <u>laughed</u> and <u>cried</u> when we <u>saw</u> that movie.

12. The woman <u>wore</u> a beautiful diamond necklace.

13. I <u>stained</u> my new shirt when I <u>spilled</u> the paint.

14. The tree <u>swayed</u> and <u>bent</u> in the strong wind.

© Carson-Dellosa CD-3760   49

Name _____ Skill: Verbs

Rule
A **verb** is a word that shows action. The underlined words are verbs.
The boy ran to the field to play soccer.

Underline every verb in each sentence.

1. Justin was so tired he <u>yawned</u>.

2. That watermelon <u>weighs</u> fifteen pounds!

3. That star <u>twinkles</u> brighter than the rest.

4. She <u>received</u> a letter today.

5. Denise <u>pinched</u> herself to <u>see</u> if she was awake.

6. He <u>offered</u> some candy to his friends.

7. The horse <u>halted</u> in front of the bridge.

8. The tiny plant <u>froze</u> when snow <u>covered</u> it.

9. The children <u>crowded</u> into the small room.

10. The angry bird <u>squawked</u> at the stranger.

11. The campfire <u>crackled</u> and <u>popped</u> cheerfully.

12. Ralph's dog <u>barked</u> and <u>growled</u> at the cat.

13. Joey <u>likes</u> to <u>read</u> books about cars.

14. Mrs. Kincaid <u>collects</u> dolls.

© Carson-Dellosa CD-3760   50

Name _____ Skill: Verbs

Rule
A **verb** is a word that shows action. The underlined words are verbs.
The boy ran to the field to play soccer.

Underline every verb in each sentence.

1. Mr. Winn <u>admired</u> the new red car.

2. Tyrone cautiously <u>approached</u> the dog.

3. The birds <u>bathed</u> happily in the cool water.

4. <u>Correct</u> the answers you <u>got</u> wrong on this paper.

5. The doctor carefully <u>examined</u> the cut.

6. The woman <u>stared</u> at the photograph for a long time.

7. Bryan <u>frowned</u> when his pencil <u>broke</u>.

8. <u>Honk</u> the car horn when you are ready.

9. It is important to <u>obey</u> the rules.

10. Your handwriting <u>improves</u> with practice.

11. Sylvia <u>drove</u> and Carmen <u>watched</u> the street signs.

12. Calvin <u>jumped</u> when the book <u>fell</u> to the floor.

13. Amanda <u>wants</u> to <u>buy</u> a sweater for her friend.

14. The yellow flowers <u>bloomed</u> early this year.

© Carson-Dellosa CD-3760   51

Name _____ Skill: Verbs

Rule
A **verb** is a word that shows action. The underlined words are verbs.
The boy ran to the field to play soccer.

Underline every verb in each sentence.

1. The plumber will <u>mend</u> the broken pipe.

2. <u>Grind</u> the coffee beans and <u>make</u> a pot of coffee for me.

3. My knee <u>jerked</u> when you <u>hit</u> it.

4. It is time to <u>harvest</u> the pumpkins!

5. Please do not <u>force</u> me to <u>say</u> that.

6. We will <u>decorate</u> this room for the party.

7. Marc <u>arrived</u> at work at one o'clock.

8. I <u>carved</u> the turkey last year.

9. I am sorry to <u>disappoint</u> you, but we can't <u>go</u> now.

10. <u>Fasten</u> the snaps on your coat because it is cold out!

11. The cow <u>munched</u> on the grass in the field.

12. Justin's eyes <u>sparkled</u> as he <u>told</u> us the joke.

13. The snow <u>fell</u> gently on the trees and bushes.

14. The librarian <u>frowned</u> when she <u>heard</u> us <u>talking</u> so loudly.

© Carson-Dellosa CD-3760   52

Answer Key

Name _____   Skill: Adjectives

Rule
An **adjective** is a word that describes a noun or pronoun.
Playful is an adjective that could describe the noun, *puppy*.

Read the sentences and choices below. For each sentence, write the correct adjective in the blank.

1. The _____ **precious** _____ jewel was very expensive!
   precious   pint   plank

2. Wear a _____ **waterproof** _____ coat in the rain.
   waiting   waterproof   watch

3. The _____ **noisy** _____ children played in the park.
   night   need   noisy

4. There were _____ **forty** _____ marbles in the bag.
   forty   flip   fly

5. The _____ **grumpy** _____ old man frowned.
   grumpy   greet   grow

6. That puppy has _____ **soft** _____ fur.
   store   sell   soft

7. The _____ **jolly** _____ clown made us laugh.
   jelly   jolly   jar

8. The _____ **green** _____ grass looked cool and inviting.
   green   grab   gain

9. My _____ **cozy** _____ blanket feels great on cool nights.
   cloud   cozy   cramp

10. The _____ **blind** _____ bat almost flew into a tree!
    band   bend   blind

© Carson-Dellosa CD-3760   53

Name _____   Skill: Adjectives

Rule
An **adjective** is a word that describes a noun or pronoun.
Playful is an adjective that could describe the noun, *puppy*.

Read the sentences and choices below. For each sentence, write the correct adjective in the blank.

1. The _____ **crisp** _____ apples made a tasty pie!
   cram   crisp   cry

2. Her _____ **golden** _____ curls were shining in the sun.
   golden   glad   grind

3. The _____ **frozen** _____ pie was too hard to eat.
   find   flower   frozen

4. The _____ **lonesome** _____ puppy whined for its mother.
   limped   lonesome   lamp

5. A _____ **curious** _____ monkey tried to open the cage.
   call   curious   crowd

6. I was _____ **nervous** _____ before the recital.
   nervous   nap   niece

7. The puppy has _____ **floppy** _____ ears.
   floppy   finish   fresh

8. That _____ **old** _____ mine is too dangerous to play near.
   out   operate   old

9. The _____ **bumpy** _____ road made the car bounce.
   bean   bumpy   blind

10. There were _____ **eleven** _____ girls and six boys at the party.
    elf   ever   eleven

© Carson-Dellosa CD-3760   54

Name _____   Skill: Adjectives

Rule
An **adjective** is a word that describes a noun or pronoun.
Playful is an adjective that could describe the noun, *puppy*.

Read the sentences and choices below. For each sentence, write the correct adjective in the blank.

1. Is your number _____ **odd** _____ or even?
   old   odd   open

2. I would like a _____ **thick** _____ , juicy steak.
   three   that   thick

3. Will you help me lift this _____ **heavy** _____ box?
   heavy   hold   haste

4. Otters are _____ **playful** _____ animals.
   penny   paying   playful

5. The _____ **distant** _____ town looked far away.
   distant   drive   drip

6. Myron was _____ **anxious** _____ to start the party.
   anxious   ants   actual

7. The _____ **thirsty** _____ boy drank six glasses of water.
   think   thirty   thirsty

8. That _____ **purple** _____ hat is beautiful!
   polite   puddle   purple

9. Jose is _____ **thirty** _____ years old.
   thirty   third   thankful

10. The cat settled down in its _____ **snug** _____ new bed.
    snarled   snug   several

© Carson-Dellosa CD-3760   55

Name _____   Skill: Adjectives

Rule
An **adjective** is a word that describes a noun or pronoun.
Playful is an adjective that could describe the noun, *puppy*.

Read the sentences and choices below. For each sentence, write the correct adjective in the blank.

1. The _____ **shrill** _____ scream upset me!
   shell   shy   shrill

2. I have _____ **ten** _____ toes.
   ten   tank   tart

3. I have _____ **white** _____ sheets on my bed.
   walnut   white   worse

4. I used a _____ **damp** _____ rag to wipe up the mess.
   damp   down   dark

5. That _____ **rude** _____ girl knocked me down!
   red   ripe   rude

6. The _____ **peaceful** _____ day made me sleepy.
   pink   plume   peaceful

7. We had a _____ **marvelous** _____ time at your party!
   mashed   marvelous   modern

8. The _____ **handsome** _____ man smiled warmly at the girl.
   handsome   hook   handful

9. The _____ **lazy** _____ boy would not clean his room.
   leopard   liquid   lazy

10. A _____ **plastic** _____ bag can be very useful!
    plastic   parent   pumping

© Carson-Dellosa CD-3760   56

Answer Key

Name _____   Skill: Subject

Rule

The **simple subject** is a noun or pronoun that tells whom or what the sentence is about.
The **complete subject** includes the simple subject and all the words that tell more about it.

The white cat slept on the pillow.
The simple subject is *cat* and the complete subject is *The white cat.*

Underline the complete subject of each sentence.

1. <u>Mark Brown</u> went on a trip with his family.
2. <u>They</u> rented a trailer and drove to California.
3. <u>The family</u> drove through the mountains.
4. <u>The mountains</u> were tall and beautiful.
5. <u>Clouds</u> covered the tops of the tallest mountains!
6. <u>The Brown family</u> also camped in a few parks.
7. <u>Their trailer</u> kept them safe from wild animals.
8. <u>A bear</u> was in their campsite one night!
9. <u>Raccoons</u> tried to get into the food supply.
10. <u>The animals</u> were never a real threat to the family, though.
11. <u>Mark</u> took many pictures of all the things they saw.
12. <u>The pictures</u> were a good reminder of that wonderful trip.

Write your own subject for each sentence.

1. <u>Answers will vary.</u> ate cookies and ice cream.
2. _____ swam in the pool.
3. _____ will take us to school.
4. _____ watched the baby.

© Carson-Dellosa CD-3760   57

Name _____   Skill: Subject

Rule

The **simple subject** is a noun or pronoun that tells whom or what the sentence is about.
The **complete subject** includes the simple subject and all the words that tell more about it.

The white cat slept on the pillow.
The simple subject is *cat* and the complete subject is *The white cat.*

Underline the complete subject of each sentence.

1. <u>A noun</u> is a person, place, or thing.
2. <u>Verbs</u> are words that show action or being.
3. <u>People</u> use nouns and verbs together to make sentences.
4. <u>Adjectives</u> can be used to tell more about nouns or pronouns.
5. <u>Adverbs</u> tell more about the verb.
6. <u>A sentence</u> tells a complete thought.
7. <u>A sentence</u> only needs a subject and a predicate.
8. <u>The subject</u> is the noun that the sentence is about.
9. <u>The predicate</u> tells what the subject is doing.
10. <u>Other words</u> in the sentence tell more about the subject and predicate.
11. <u>You</u> can find the subject if you try.
12. <u>It</u> isn't very hard to do!

Write your own subject for each sentence.

1. <u>Answers will vary.</u> went to the movie.
2. _____ plays the drums in the band.
3. _____ understands that story.
4. _____ is a very nice person.

© Carson-Dellosa CD-3760   58

Name _____   Skill: Subject

Rule

The **simple subject** is a noun or pronoun that tells whom or what the sentence is about.
The **complete subject** includes the simple subject and all the words that tell more about it.

The white cat slept on the pillow.
The simple subject is *cat* and the complete subject is *The white cat.*

Underline the complete subject of each sentence.

1. <u>Africa</u> is one of the continents of the Earth.
2. <u>Africa</u> has many different countries.
3. <u>Kenya</u> is a country in eastern Africa.
4. <u>The southeast coast of Africa</u> borders the Indian Ocean.
5. <u>Kenya</u> has a famous park.
6. <u>Mt. Elgon National Park</u> is the name of the park.
7. <u>It</u> is a great place to watch elephants.
8. <u>Large lions</u> live there, too.
9. <u>Many visitors</u> come to see the animals each year.
10. <u>A hotel</u> was built near a watering hole for the animals.
11. <u>People</u> can watch the wild animals right from their rooms!
12. <u>The animals</u> like to watch the people, too!

Write your own subject for each sentence.

1. <u>Answers will vary.</u> is my favorite pet.
2. _____ ate pickles and peanut butter.
3. _____ like to listen to music.
4. _____ rode the wagon to town.

© Carson-Dellosa CD-3760   59

Name _____   Skill: Subject

Rule

The **simple subject** is a noun or pronoun that tells whom or what the sentence is about.
The **complete subject** includes the simple subject and all the words that tell more about it.

The white cat slept on the pillow.
The simple subject is *cat* and the complete subject is *The white cat.*

Underline the complete subject of each sentence.

1. <u>Susan</u> plays flute in the school band.
2. <u>Two mice</u> stored seeds in the garden.
3. <u>Chess</u> is my favorite game.
4. <u>The leaves</u> on the trees are turning color.
5. <u>Janice</u> read a book that was funny.
6. <u>Those brown socks</u> do not match your pants.
7. <u>Carol</u> lost her sweater at the party.
8. <u>The Rodriguez family</u> has a yellow van.
9. <u>Penny</u> went to the park with her friends after school.
10. <u>That science project</u> is the best one in third grade!
11. <u>The brown and white horse</u> is running across the field.
12. <u>The rain</u> fell all afternoon.

Write your own subject for each sentence.

1. <u>Answers will vary.</u> bought a new pair of skates.
2. _____ ate at a restaurant.
3. _____ washed its paws in the river.
4. _____ was speeding down the street.

© Carson-Dellosa CD-3760   60

Answer Key

Name _____   Skill: Predicate

Rule

The **simple predicate** is a verb that tells what the subject did or what was done to the subject.
The **complete predicate** includes the verb and all the words that tell more about it.

The white cat slept on the pillow.

The simple predicate is *slept* and the complete predicate is *slept on the pillow.*

Underline the complete predicate of each sentence.

1. The cows and horses <u>stayed in the barn during the storm</u>.
2. The small brown fox <u>ran into the hole</u>.
3. Alex and his brother <u>played all afternoon</u>.
4. Uncle Vinnie <u>sent a postcard from Italy</u>.
5. My mother and father <u>are going to the store</u>.
6. The large, green truck <u>rolled down the highway</u>.
7. It <u>was snowing last week</u>.
8. My sister <u>baby-sits for the neighbors</u>.
9. We <u>will eat dinner</u>.
10. I <u>danced in the play</u>.
11. The oranges and lemons <u>grew in the orchard</u>.
12. Rusty and Terry <u>took the test yesterday</u>.

Write your own predicate for each sentence.

1. Jonas and Kristie **Answers will vary.** _____ .
2. Those rabbits _____ .
3. The desk in the front row _____ .
4. All of the children _____ .

Name _____   Skill: Predicate

Rule

The **simple predicate** is a verb that tells what the subject did or what was done to the subject.
The **complete predicate** includes the verb and all the words that tell more about it.

The white cat slept on the pillow.

The simple predicate is *slept* and the complete predicate is *slept on the pillow.*

Underline the complete predicate of each sentence.

1. I <u>like the colors yellow and blue</u>.
2. My teacher, Miss Winter, <u>brought a gerbil for the class</u>.
3. Kevin <u>wants to be a doctor someday</u>.
4. The telephone <u>rang seven times</u>!
5. That little boy <u>lost his shoe this morning</u>.
6. Mike <u>cut his hair very short</u>.
7. The thief <u>stole the diamond necklace</u>.
8. The big brown bear <u>protected her cub</u>.
9. The audience <u>clapped at the end of the play</u>.
10. My mother <u>writes books</u>.
11. The man with the beard <u>drives a truck</u>.
12. Brian <u>held the baby bird</u>.

Write your own predicate for each sentence.

1. The big brown box **Answers will vary.** _____ .
2. Six boys _____ .
3. My younger brother _____ .
4. When you smile, you _____ .

Name _____   Skill: Predicate

Rule

A **simple predicate** is a verb that tells what the subject did or what was done to the subject.
A **complete predicate** includes the verb and all the words that tell more about it.

The white cat slept on the pillow.

The simple predicate is *slept* and the complete predicate is *slept on the pillow.*

Underline the complete predicate of each sentence.

1. The marching band <u>plays in every parade</u>.
2. I <u>watched television until bedtime</u>.
3. The sad little girl <u>cried</u>.
4. Lamont <u>jumped over the fence</u>.
5. The airplane <u>landed in Chicago</u>.
6. The boat with the blue sails <u>tipped over in the storm</u>.
7. Liz <u>covered her head during the scary part of the movie</u>.
8. That photographer <u>takes great pictures</u>!
9. The wind <u>blew over the picnic table</u>.
10. We <u>built a sand castle at the beach</u>.
11. We <u>ate lots of ice cream</u>.
12. Ben <u>walks to school</u>.

Write your own predicate for each sentence.

1. Before school I **Answers will vary.** _____ .
2. The zebras and monkeys _____ .
3. My class _____ .
4. The computer in the office _____ .

Name _____   Skill: Predicate

Rule

A **simple predicate** is a verb that tells what the subject did or what was done to the subject.
A **complete predicate** includes the verb and all the words that tell more about it.

The white cat slept on the pillow.

The simple predicate is *slept* and the complete predicate is *slept on the pillow.*

Underline the complete predicate of each sentence.

1. Pamela <u>will write six letters tonight</u>.
2. The kitten <u>hides under the couch</u>.
3. My best friend <u>moved to another state</u>.
4. The wild animals <u>roamed the forest</u>.
5. Jerry <u>enjoyed the movie</u>.
6. Randy and Karl <u>swim in the lake</u>.
7. My aunt's pizza <u>tastes wonderful</u>!
8. The two friends <u>sat together on the bus</u>.
9. George <u>picked blueberries yesterday</u>.
10. My dad <u>built my tree house</u>.
11. The yellow and white daisies <u>swayed in the breeze</u>.
12. Carlos <u>saw the accident last week</u>.

Write your own predicate for each sentence.

1. Brittany's cat **Answers will vary.** _____ .
2. My elbow _____ .
3. The package with the green bow _____ .
4. The mail carrier _____ .

Answer Key

Name _____ Skill: Fragments

Rule

A **sentence** is a group of words that expresses a complete thought.
A **fragment** is an incomplete sentence because it does not express a complete thought.
Fragments: *Anna and Beth.* (missing a predicate that tells what happened)
Went swimming. (missing a subject that tells who)
Sentence: *Anna and Beth went swimming.*

Write **S** if the words below form a sentence and **F** if they are a fragment.

F 1. The picture on the wall.
S 2. We rented skates.
F 3. Bowling in the afternoon.
F 4. The curious little kitten.
S 5. Keep the cookies separate from the doughnuts.
S 6. Alice and Glenda wrote the play.
F 7. Acted as if they were really scared.
S 8. The panda ate bamboo shoots.
F 9. Pedro and his cousin, Juan.
F 10. Running through the neighbor's yard.
S 11. The big moving van came down our street.
F 12. Called hello to all our friends.

Add words to make each fragment a sentence.

1. Storms are **Answers will vary.** .
2. _____ racing each other.
3. A very loud noise _____ .
4. _____ playing in the warm sunshine.

© Carson-Dellosa CD-3760   65

Name _____ Skill: Fragments

Rule

A **sentence** is a group of words that expresses a complete thought.
A **fragment** is an incomplete sentence because it does not express a complete thought.
Fragments: *Anna and Beth.* (missing a predicate that tells what happened)
Went swimming. (missing a subject that tells who)
Sentence: *Anna and Beth went swimming.*

Write **S** if the words below form a sentence and **F** if they are a fragment.

F 1. The moment we have been waiting for.
S 2. The queen's gown was lovely.
F 3. Across the street and in the yard.
S 4. Albert waited quietly.
F 5. The Empire State Building and other buildings.
F 6. Perhaps after dinner.
S 7. We held our breath and waited for the answer.
F 8. A wild look in his eyes.
S 9. Miguel hid behind the tree.
F 10. The nicest looking cake I had ever seen.
F 11. Through the fields and into the barnyard.
S 12. Francine waved to us.

Add words to make each fragment a sentence.

1. From the front of the boat **Answers will vary.** .
2. _____ eating grapes.
3. The whole group _____ .
4. _____ picking flowers.

© Carson-Dellosa CD-3760   66

Name _____ Skill: Capitalization

Rule

Remember to use **capital letters** for:
• the first word in a sentence   • the pronoun "I"
• proper nouns   • important words in book and movie titles

Each sentence below has one or more capitalization mistakes. Write each sentence correctly on the line below it.

1. My uncle's name is edward.
   My uncle's name is Edward.
2. the line for the movie was very long.
   The line for the movie was very long.
3. Huey and i are best friends.
   Huey and I are best friends.
4. We will study the country of ireland.
   We will study the country of Ireland.
5. I am reading a book called the little prince.
   I am reading a book called The Little Prince.
6. Lucille and margaret brought flowers.
   Lucille and Margaret brought flowers.
7. James just got back from florida.
   James just got back from Florida.
8. The name of my doctor is paula milne.
   The name of my doctor is Paula Milne.
9. we can play after school.
   We can play after school.
10. The nile river is the longest river in the world.
    The Nile River is the longest river in the world.
11. The teacher just finished reading charlotte's web.
    The teacher just finished reading Charlotte's Web.
12. joey went to texas last summer.
    Joey went to Texas last summer.

© Carson-Dellosa CD-3760   67

Name _____ Skill: Capitalization

Rule

Remember to use **capital letters** for:
• the first word in a sentence   • the pronoun "I"
• proper nouns   • important words in book and movie titles

Each sentence below has one or more capitalization mistakes. Write each sentence correctly on the line below it.

1. the ugly duckling is my favorite fairy tale.
   The Ugly Duckling is my favorite fairy tale.
2. when i clap my hands, we will line up.
   When I clap my hands, we will line up.
3. I like to go shopping with maude and kathy.
   I like to go shopping with Maude and Kathy.
4. Have you ever been to africa?
   Have you ever been to Africa?
5. My dad just read a novel called treasure island.
   My dad just read a novel called Treasure Island.
6. i would like to visit france some day.
   I would like to visit France some day.
7. We flew to new york for thanksgiving.
   We just flew to New York for Thanksgiving.
8. mexico is a country in north america.
   Mexico is a country in North America.
9. the baseball broke the window.
   The baseball broke the window.
10. We took a trip to california last august.
    We took a trip to California last August.
11. My birthday is on tuesday this year.
    My birthday is on Tuesday this year.
12. It often snows in december.
    It often snows in December.

© Carson-Dellosa CD-3760   68

Answer Key

Name _____ Skill: Addition Facts
Add.

#		#		#		#		#		#		#	
1.	3 + 2 = 5	2.	7 + 0 = 7	3.	9 + 4 = 13	4.	3 + 7 = 10	5.	8 + 8 = 16	6.	5 + 2 = 7	7.	4 + 7 = 11
8.	1 + 2 = 3	9.	4 + 7 = 11	10.	3 + 4 = 7	11.	5 + 9 = 14	12.	9 + 8 = 17	13.	2 + 1 = 3	14.	8 + 3 = 11
15.	0 + 9 = 9	16.	6 + 5 = 11	17.	8 + 5 = 13	18.	4 + 7 = 11	19.	2 + 2 = 4	20.	5 + 3 = 8	21.	3 + 8 = 11
22.	8 + 0 = 8	23.	7 + 4 = 11	24.	4 + 5 = 9	25.	1 + 9 = 10	26.	9 + 7 = 16	27.	5 + 3 = 8	28.	3 + 6 = 9
29.	6 + 4 = 10	30.	9 + 9 = 18	31.	8 + 8 = 16	32.	3 + 3 = 6	33.	8 + 2 = 10	34.	2 + 1 = 3	35.	7 + 6 = 13
36.	10 + 2 = 12	37.	0 + 9 = 9	38.	2 + 0 = 2	39.	6 + 5 = 11	40.	4 + 1 = 5	41.	9 + 7 = 16	42.	7 + 3 = 10
43.	6 + 9 = 15	44.	7 + 6 = 13	45.	9 + 6 = 15	46.	6 + 2 = 8	47.	5 + 5 = 10	48.	5 + 4 = 9	49.	10 + 1 = 11

Name _____ Skill: Two-Digit Addition
Add.

#		#		#		#		#		#		#	
1.	33 + 21 = 54	2.	70 + 20 = 90	3.	39 + 40 = 79	4.	31 + 57 = 88	5.	28 + 11 = 39	6.	56 + 23 = 79	7.	44 + 23 = 67
8.	71 + 25 = 96	9.	42 + 47 = 89	10.	63 + 14 = 77	11.	50 + 17 = 67	12.	29 + 70 = 99	13.	82 + 16 = 98	14.	38 + 31 = 69
15.	70 + 19 = 89	16.	46 + 12 = 58	17.	70 + 14 = 84	18.	54 + 14 = 68	19.	20 + 30 = 50	20.	25 + 34 = 59	21.	53 + 16 = 69
22.	28 + 50 = 78	23.	17 + 42 = 59	24.	24 + 50 = 74	25.	81 + 11 = 92	26.	33 + 23 = 56	27.	51 + 35 = 86	28.	13 + 66 = 79
29.	56 + 41 = 97	30.	19 + 70 = 89	31.	34 + 12 = 46	32.	13 + 43 = 56	33.	58 + 20 = 78	34.	23 + 25 = 48	35.	47 + 22 = 69
36.	10 + 24 = 34	37.	37 + 20 = 57	38.	26 + 43 = 69	39.	61 + 17 = 78	40.	44 + 34 = 78	41.	29 + 40 = 69	42.	72 + 13 = 85
43.	60 + 29 = 89	44.	57 + 11 = 68	45.	49 + 50 = 99	46.	26 + 20 = 46	47.	52 + 25 = 77	48.	53 + 41 = 94	49.	35 + 21 = 56

Name _____ Skill: Two-Digit Addition
Add.

#		#		#		#		#		#		#	
1.	53 + 29 = 82	2.	17 + 55 = 72	3.	46 + 27 = 73	4.	38 + 49 = 87	5.	45 + 28 = 73	6.	86 + 64 = 150	7.	27 + 39 = 66
8.	99 + 59 = 158	9.	23 + 78 = 101	10.	38 + 57 = 95	11.	85 + 53 = 138	12.	91 + 46 = 137	13.	33 + 19 = 52	14.	84 + 37 = 121
15.	29 + 61 = 90	16.	92 + 48 = 140	17.	22 + 89 = 111	18.	45 + 73 = 118	19.	74 + 18 = 92	20.	96 + 33 = 129	21.	26 + 77 = 103
22.	96 + 58 = 154	23.	26 + 86 = 112	24.	74 + 38 = 112	25.	82 + 24 = 106	26.	99 + 47 = 146	27.	46 + 28 = 74	28.	76 + 25 = 101
29.	19 + 41 = 60	30.	58 + 63 = 121	31.	63 + 59 = 122	32.	81 + 73 = 154	33.	72 + 28 = 100	34.	35 + 66 = 101	35.	27 + 28 = 55
36.	48 + 57 = 105	37.	74 + 63 = 137	38.	61 + 56 = 117	39.	70 + 54 = 124	40.	93 + 28 = 121	41.	65 + 49 = 114	42.	29 + 79 = 108
43.	36 + 77 = 113	44.	77 + 34 = 111	45.	84 + 63 = 147	46.	25 + 57 = 82	47.	89 + 21 = 110	48.	58 + 47 = 105	49.	34 + 48 = 82

Name _____ Skill: Three-Digit Addition
Add.

#		#		#		#		#		#		#	
1.	303 + 214 = 517	2.	870 + 189 = 1,059	3.	408 + 159 = 567	4.	327 + 196 = 523	5.	417 + 125 = 542	6.	730 + 197 = 927	7.	344 + 523 = 867
8.	751 + 225 = 976	9.	400 + 127 = 527	10.	111 + 345 = 456	11.	250 + 178 = 428	12.	219 + 470 = 689	13.	382 + 160 = 542	14.	348 + 436 = 784
15.	709 + 189 = 898	16.	522 + 157 = 679	17.	398 + 145 = 543	18.	270 + 134 = 404	19.	520 + 177 = 697	20.	254 + 384 = 638	21.	953 + 119 = 1,072
22.	428 + 150 = 578	23.	197 + 402 = 599	24.	724 + 150 = 874	25.	181 + 199 = 380	26.	533 + 238 = 771	27.	451 + 315 = 766	28.	613 + 178 = 791
29.	357 + 417 = 774	30.	519 + 170 = 689	31.	834 + 196 = 1,030	32.	313 + 488 = 801	33.	558 + 184 = 742	34.	687 + 139 = 826	35.	901 + 149 = 1,050
36.	410 + 291 = 701	37.	737 + 288 = 1,025	38.	426 + 497 = 923	39.	166 + 617 = 783	40.	404 + 395 = 799	41.	259 + 450 = 709	42.	272 + 438 = 710
43.	106 + 329 = 435	44.	857 + 241 = 1,098	45.	849 + 154 = 1,003	46.	426 + 208 = 634	47.	572 + 259 = 831	48.	553 + 347 = 900	49.	436 + 574 = 1,010

Answer Key

Worksheet 1 — Skill: Subtraction Facts

Name _____

Subtract.

#		#		#		#	
1.	3 − 2 = 1	2.	7 − 0 = 7	3.	9 − 4 = 5	4.	7 − 3 = 4
5.	8 − 8 = 0	6.	5 − 2 = 3	7.	9 − 4 = 5		
8.	4 − 2 = 2	9.	9 − 7 = 2	10.	10 − 4 = 6	11.	6 − 1 = 5
12.	9 − 8 = 1	13.	2 − 1 = 1	14.	8 − 3 = 5		
15.	10 − 9 = 1	16.	12 − 5 = 7	17.	11 − 4 = 7	18.	10 − 7 = 3
19.	2 − 2 = 0	20.	15 − 6 = 9	21.	13 − 8 = 5		
22.	8 − 4 = 4	23.	7 − 2 = 5	24.	14 − 5 = 9	25.	11 − 9 = 2
26.	17 − 9 = 8	27.	5 − 3 = 2	28.	13 − 6 = 7		
29.	14 − 6 = 8	30.	9 − 9 = 0	31.	14 − 7 = 7	32.	13 − 9 = 4
33.	8 − 2 = 6	34.	12 − 9 = 3	35.	16 − 7 = 9		
36.	10 − 2 = 8	37.	18 − 9 = 9	38.	12 − 5 = 7	39.	16 − 7 = 9
40.	14 − 5 = 9	41.	9 − 7 = 2	42.	17 − 8 = 9		
43.	10 − 6 = 4	44.	7 − 6 = 1	45.	9 − 6 = 3	46.	6 − 2 = 4
47.	15 − 8 = 7	48.	17 − 9 = 8	49.	11 − 6 = 5		

73

Worksheet 2 — Skill: Two-Digit Subtraction

Name _____

Subtract.

#		#		#		#	
1.	30 − 10 = 20	2.	70 − 40 = 30	3.	90 − 40 = 50	4.	60 − 30 = 30
5.	80 − 80 = 0	6.	50 − 20 = 30	7.	90 − 10 = 80		
8.	40 − 20 = 20	9.	90 − 70 = 20	10.	50 − 40 = 10	11.	60 − 10 = 50
12.	90 − 80 = 10	13.	20 − 10 = 10	14.	80 − 30 = 50		
15.	55 − 43 = 12	16.	72 − 50 = 22	17.	88 − 41 = 47	18.	33 − 22 = 11
19.	72 − 32 = 40	20.	75 − 64 = 11	21.	99 − 48 = 51		
22.	87 − 46 = 41	23.	78 − 24 = 54	24.	83 − 51 = 32	25.	69 − 19 = 50
26.	76 − 45 = 31	27.	58 − 30 = 28	28.	66 − 62 = 4		
29.	72 − 61 = 11	30.	98 − 46 = 52	31.	33 − 12 = 21	32.	84 − 23 = 61
33.	88 − 72 = 16	34.	48 − 32 = 16	35.	76 − 51 = 25		
36.	95 − 23 = 72	37.	80 − 40 = 40	38.	67 − 51 = 16	39.	82 − 70 = 12
40.	96 − 53 = 43	41.	79 − 17 = 62	42.	87 − 47 = 40		
43.	85 − 60 = 25	44.	70 − 60 = 10	45.	93 − 60 = 33	46.	57 − 23 = 34
47.	77 − 17 = 60	48.	84 − 62 = 22	49.	56 − 41 = 15		

74

Worksheet 3 — Skill: Two-Digit Subtraction

Name _____

Subtract.

#		#		#		#	
1.	91 − 56 = 35	2.	52 − 49 = 3	3.	43 − 38 = 5	4.	71 − 34 = 37
5.	75 − 46 = 29	6.	84 − 47 = 37	7.	61 − 12 = 49		
8.	86 − 58 = 28	9.	90 − 29 = 61	10.	42 − 28 = 14	11.	94 − 66 = 28
12.	62 − 49 = 13	13.	55 − 17 = 38	14.	41 − 25 = 16		
15.	86 − 39 = 47	16.	34 − 18 = 16	17.	73 − 38 = 35	18.	44 − 15 = 29
19.	73 − 25 = 48	20.	58 − 39 = 19	21.	52 − 24 = 28		
22.	38 − 19 = 19	23.	46 − 28 = 18	24.	53 − 28 = 25	25.	95 − 48 = 47
26.	84 − 27 = 57	27.	64 − 39 = 25	28.	92 − 59 = 33		
29.	87 − 38 = 49	30.	74 − 25 = 49	31.	67 − 38 = 29	32.	71 − 64 = 7
33.	83 − 28 = 55	34.	41 − 34 = 7	35.	71 − 42 = 29		
36.	93 − 75 = 18	37.	84 − 19 = 65	38.	82 − 73 = 9	39.	84 − 37 = 47
40.	66 − 48 = 18	41.	75 − 27 = 48	42.	54 − 39 = 15		
43.	75 − 17 = 58	44.	47 − 18 = 29	45.	40 − 29 = 11	46.	61 − 23 = 38
47.	54 − 38 = 16	48.	81 − 27 = 54	49.	93 − 56 = 37		

75

Worksheet 4 — Skill: Three-Digit Subtraction

Name _____

Subtract.

#		#		#		#	
1.	326 − 285 = 41	2.	972 − 609 = 363	3.	685 − 246 = 439	4.	518 − 329 = 189
5.	741 − 362 = 379	6.	438 − 258 = 180	7.	371 − 283 = 88		
8.	529 − 482 = 47	9.	625 − 407 = 218	10.	514 − 126 = 388	11.	664 − 278 = 386
12.	742 − 467 = 275	13.	200 − 158 = 42	14.	634 − 277 = 357		
15.	423 − 285 = 138	16.	222 − 153 = 69	17.	435 − 166 = 269	18.	628 − 499 = 129
19.	757 − 178 = 579	20.	637 − 388 = 249	21.	423 − 285 = 138		
22.	533 − 240 = 293	23.	415 − 196 = 219	24.	382 − 175 = 207	25.	632 − 377 = 255
26.	585 − 423 = 162	27.	778 − 439 = 339	28.	165 − 130 = 35		
29.	623 − 194 = 429	30.	900 − 309 = 591	31.	722 − 317 = 405	32.	377 − 186 = 191
33.	871 − 384 = 487	34.	628 − 300 = 328	35.	454 − 279 = 175		
36.	990 − 731 = 259	37.	818 − 693 = 125	38.	572 − 335 = 237	39.	951 − 357 = 594
40.	825 − 469 = 356	41.	771 − 217 = 554	42.	943 − 761 = 182		
43.	407 − 328 = 79	44.	431 − 298 = 133	45.	906 − 682 = 224	46.	486 − 297 = 189
47.	615 − 288 = 327	48.	883 − 227 = 656	49.	725 − 387 = 338		

76

Answer Key

Panel 1 (page 77)

Name _____ Skill: Multiplication Facts
Multiply.

#		#		#		#		#		#		#	
1.	3 ×2 = 6	2.	7 ×0 = 0	3.	9 ×3 = 27	4.	3 ×1 = 3	5.	8 ×2 = 16	6.	5 ×2 = 10	7.	3 ×7 = 21
8.	1 ×2 = 2	9.	0 ×8 = 0	10.	3 ×4 = 12	11.	2 ×9 = 18	12.	9 ×0 = 0	13.	2 ×1 = 2	14.	8 ×3 = 24
15.	9 ×1 = 9	16.	6 ×3 = 18	17.	0 ×4 = 0	18.	5 ×1 = 5	19.	2 ×2 = 4	20.	5 ×3 = 15	21.	3 ×2 = 6
22.	8 ×0 = 0	23.	8 ×3 = 24	24.	1 ×5 = 5	25.	3 ×9 = 27	26.	9 ×2 = 18	27.	5 ×0 = 0	28.	3 ×6 = 18
29.	6 ×0 = 0	30.	9 ×3 = 27	31.	1 ×7 = 7	32.	3 ×3 = 9	33.	8 ×2 = 16	34.	2 ×1 = 2	35.	7 ×2 = 14
36.	10 ×2 = 20	37.	0 ×9 = 0	38.	2 ×0 = 0	39.	3 ×5 = 15	40.	0 ×1 = 0	41.	9 ×3 = 27	42.	8 ×2 = 16
43.	6 ×3 = 18	44.	7 ×1 = 7	45.	2 ×6 = 12	46.	4 ×2 = 8	47.	5 ×0 = 0	48.	1 ×4 = 4	49.	2 ×9 = 18

© Carson-Dellosa CD-3760   77

Panel 2 (page 78)

Name _____ Skill: Multiplication Facts
Multiply.

#		#		#		#		#		#		#	
1.	3 ×4 = 12	2.	7 ×5 = 35	3.	6 ×3 = 18	4.	3 ×7 = 21	5.	8 ×5 = 40	6.	4 ×2 = 8	7.	3 ×6 = 18
8.	1 ×4 = 4	9.	0 ×5 = 0	10.	6 ×4 = 24	11.	7 ×9 = 63	12.	9 ×4 = 36	13.	5 ×1 = 5	14.	8 ×6 = 48
15.	9 ×4 = 36	16.	6 ×5 = 30	17.	0 ×6 = 0	18.	5 ×7 = 35	19.	2 ×4 = 8	20.	5 ×5 = 25	21.	3 ×6 = 18
22.	8 ×7 = 56	23.	8 ×4 = 32	24.	1 ×5 = 5	25.	6 ×9 = 54	26.	9 ×7 = 63	27.	5 ×4 = 20	28.	6 ×6 = 36
29.	6 ×6 = 36	30.	9 ×5 = 45	31.	4 ×7 = 28	32.	8 ×7 = 21	33.	8 ×5 = 40	34.	2 ×4 = 8	35.	7 ×7 = 49
36.	10 ×4 = 40	37.	4 ×1 = 4	38.	5 ×0 = 0	39.	8 ×5 = 40	40.	6 ×1 = 6	41.	9 ×6 = 54	42.	7 ×9 = 63
43.	6 ×7 = 42	44.	7 ×7 = 49	45.	7 ×6 = 42	46.	5 ×2 = 10	47.	5 ×6 = 30	48.	7 ×4 = 28	49.	2 ×8 = 16

© Carson-Dellosa CD-3760   78

Panel 3 (page 79)

Name _____ Skill: Multiplication Facts
Multiply.

#		#		#		#		#		#		#	
1.	8 ×3 = 24	2.	7 ×9 = 63	3.	10 ×3 = 30	4.	11 ×3 = 33	5.	8 ×8 = 64	6.	9 ×2 = 18	7.	10 ×7 = 70
8.	12 ×2 = 24	9.	10 ×8 = 80	10.	9 ×4 = 36	11.	8 ×9 = 72	12.	10 ×9 = 90	13.	12 ×1 = 12	14.	8 ×3 = 24
15.	12 ×9 = 108	16.	6 ×9 = 54	17.	10 ×4 = 40	18.	12 ×5 = 60	19.	10 ×2 = 20	20.	8 ×3 = 24	21.	9 ×8 = 72
22.	11 ×0 = 0	23.	8 ×3 = 24	24.	12 ×5 = 60	25.	7 ×8 = 56	26.	9 ×9 = 81	27.	10 ×3 = 30	28.	11 ×6 = 66
29.	10 ×6 = 60	30.	9 ×3 = 27	31.	11 ×7 = 77	32.	3 ×8 = 24	33.	8 ×8 = 64	34.	10 ×2 = 20	35.	7 ×9 = 63
36.	11 ×2 = 22	37.	10 ×9 = 90	38.	2 ×9 = 18	39.	8 ×5 = 40	40.	10 ×1 = 10	41.	11 ×9 = 99	42.	10 ×7 = 70
43.	11 ×6 = 66	44.	7 ×8 = 56	45.	10 ×6 = 60	46.	12 ×6 = 72	47.	5 ×9 = 45	48.	9 ×4 = 36	49.	10 ×8 = 80

© Carson-Dellosa CD-3760   79

Panel 4 (page 80)

Name _____ Skill: Division Facts
Divide.

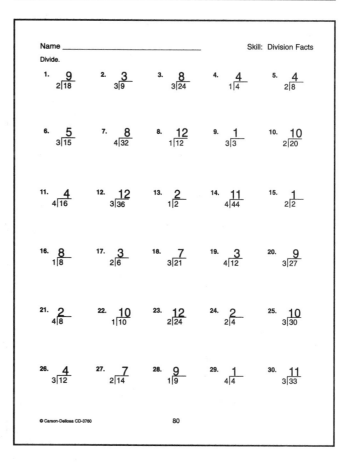

#		#		#		#		#	
1.	$2\overline{)18} = 9$	2.	$3\overline{)9} = 3$	3.	$3\overline{)24} = 8$	4.	$1\overline{)4} = 4$	5.	$2\overline{)8} = 4$
6.	$3\overline{)15} = 5$	7.	$4\overline{)32} = 8$	8.	$1\overline{)12} = 12$	9.	$3\overline{)3} = 1$	10.	$2\overline{)20} = 10$
11.	$4\overline{)16} = 4$	12.	$3\overline{)36} = 12$	13.	$1\overline{)2} = 2$	14.	$4\overline{)44} = 11$	15.	$2\overline{)2} = 1$
16.	$1\overline{)8} = 8$	17.	$2\overline{)6} = 3$	18.	$3\overline{)21} = 7$	19.	$4\overline{)12} = 3$	20.	$3\overline{)27} = 9$
21.	$4\overline{)8} = 2$	22.	$1\overline{)10} = 10$	23.	$2\overline{)24} = 12$	24.	$2\overline{)4} = 2$	25.	$3\overline{)30} = 10$
26.	$3\overline{)12} = 4$	27.	$2\overline{)14} = 7$	28.	$1\overline{)9} = 9$	29.	$4\overline{)4} = 1$	30.	$3\overline{)33} = 11$

© Carson-Dellosa CD-3760   80

Answer Key

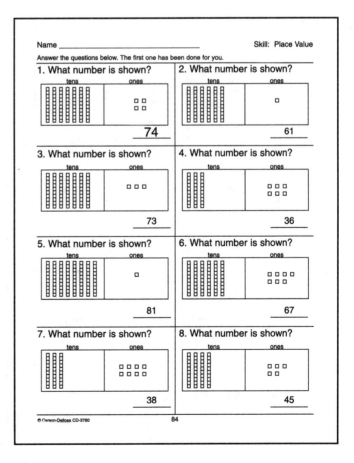

Answer Key

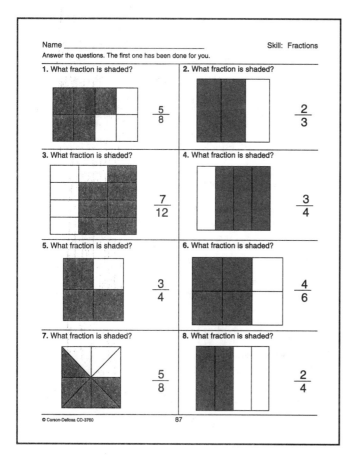
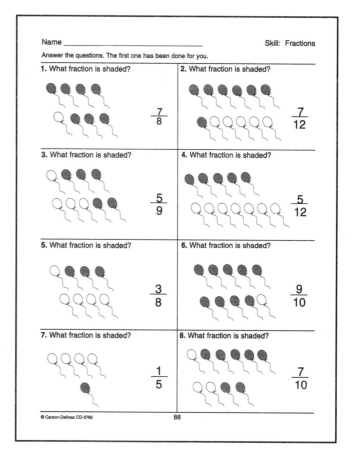

Answer Key

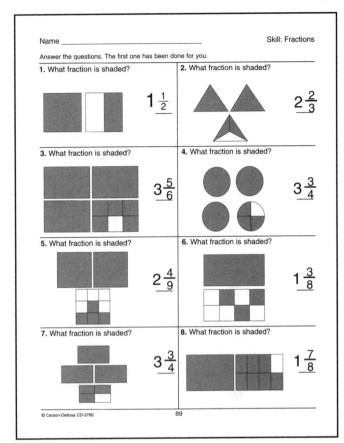

Name _____ Skill: Fractions

Answer the questions. The first one has been done for you.

1. What fraction is shaded?

$1\frac{1}{2}$

2. What fraction is shaded?

$2\frac{2}{3}$

3. What fraction is shaded?

$3\frac{5}{6}$

4. What fraction is shaded?

$3\frac{3}{4}$

5. What fraction is shaded?

$2\frac{4}{9}$

6. What fraction is shaded?

$1\frac{3}{8}$

7. What fraction is shaded?

$3\frac{3}{4}$

8. What fraction is shaded?

$1\frac{7}{8}$

© Carson-Dellosa CD-3760   89

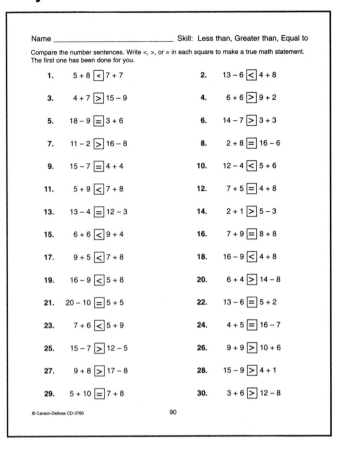

Name _____ Skill: Less than, Greater than, Equal to

Compare the number sentences. Write <, >, or = in each square to make a true math statement. The first one has been done for you.

1. $5 + 8 \boxed{<} 7 + 7$
2. $13 - 6 \boxed{<} 4 + 8$
3. $4 + 7 \boxed{>} 15 - 9$
4. $6 + 6 \boxed{>} 9 + 2$
5. $18 - 9 \boxed{=} 3 + 6$
6. $14 - 7 \boxed{>} 3 + 3$
7. $11 - 2 \boxed{>} 16 - 8$
8. $2 + 8 \boxed{=} 16 - 6$
9. $15 - 7 \boxed{=} 4 + 4$
10. $12 - 4 \boxed{<} 5 + 6$
11. $5 + 9 \boxed{<} 7 + 8$
12. $7 + 5 \boxed{=} 4 + 8$
13. $13 - 4 \boxed{=} 12 - 3$
14. $2 + 1 \boxed{>} 5 - 3$
15. $6 + 6 \boxed{<} 9 + 4$
16. $7 + 9 \boxed{=} 8 + 8$
17. $9 + 5 \boxed{<} 7 + 8$
18. $16 - 9 \boxed{<} 4 + 8$
19. $16 - 9 \boxed{<} 5 + 8$
20. $6 + 4 \boxed{>} 14 - 8$
21. $20 - 10 \boxed{=} 5 + 5$
22. $13 - 6 \boxed{=} 5 + 2$
23. $7 + 6 \boxed{<} 5 + 9$
24. $4 + 5 \boxed{=} 16 - 7$
25. $15 - 7 \boxed{>} 12 - 5$
26. $9 + 9 \boxed{>} 10 + 6$
27. $9 + 8 \boxed{>} 17 - 8$
28. $15 - 9 \boxed{>} 4 + 1$
29. $5 + 10 \boxed{=} 7 + 8$
30. $3 + 6 \boxed{>} 12 - 8$

© Carson-Dellosa CD-3760   90

Name _____ Skill: Less than, Greater than, Equal to

Compare the number sentences. Write <, >, or = in each square to make a true math statement. The first one has been done for you.

1. $11 - 6 \boxed{<} 3 + 3$
2. $2 + 6 \boxed{=} 10 - 2$
3. $17 - 8 \boxed{>} 2 + 5$
4. $14 - 6 \boxed{<} 3 + 6$
5. $16 - 8 \boxed{<} 4 + 5$
6. $5 + 8 \boxed{>} 17 - 7$
7. $6 + 7 \boxed{<} 5 + 9$
8. $13 - 9 \boxed{>} 3 + 0$
9. $12 - 8 \boxed{<} 3 + 4$
10. $4 + 2 \boxed{=} 12 - 6$
11. $17 - 9 \boxed{<} 15 - 6$
12. $5 + 5 \boxed{>} 17 - 8$
13. $1 \times 6 \boxed{=} 6 - 0$
14. $0 \times 4 \boxed{<} 4 + 0$
15. $9 + 9 \boxed{=} 6 \times 3$
16. $5 \times 2 \boxed{>} 15 - 6$
17. $10 - 5 \boxed{>} 2 \times 2$
18. $9 - 6 \boxed{<} 4 \times 2$
19. $3 \times 2 \boxed{<} 17 - 9$
20. $1 \times 9 \boxed{>} 7 + 1$
21. $2 \times 1 \boxed{<} 8 - 5$
22. $7 \times 3 \boxed{>} 9 + 9$
23. $7 \times 1 \boxed{<} 12 - 4$
24. $8 + 8 \boxed{=} 8 \times 2$
25. $15 - 8 \boxed{<} 3 \times 3$
26. $8 - 0 \boxed{>} 5 \times 0$
27. $6 \times 2 \boxed{<} 6 + 7$
28. $7 \times 1 \boxed{<} 4 + 5$
29. $7 + 8 \boxed{=} 5 \times 3$
30. $16 - 8 \boxed{=} 2 \times 4$

© Carson-Dellosa CD-3760   91

Name _____ Skill: Word Problems

Read the paragraph carefully, then answer the questions. Write **NG** (not given) if there is not enough information to answer the question.

Andrea had a busy day. She got up at 7:00 in the morning. School started at 8:00 a.m. and ended at 3:30 p.m. Right after school, Andrea went to band practice for one hour. She got home half an hour later. She ate dinner at 6:00 p.m. At 7:00 p.m. she started her homework and she finished at 9:00 p.m. She went to bed at 9:30 p.m.

1. At what time did Andrea start school?
Andrea started school at 8:00 a.m.

2. How many hours was Andrea in school?
Andrea was in school for seven and one-half hours.

3. At what time did Andrea finish band practice?
Andrea finished band practice at 4:30 p.m.

4. What time was it when Andrea got home that afternoon?
Andrea arrived home at 5:00 p.m.

5. How many hours did Andrea work on her homework?
Andrea worked for two hours on her homework.

6. At what time did she go to bed?
Andrea went to bed at 9:30 p.m.

7. At what time did Andrea eat lunch?
NG

8. How many hours was it from the time she got up until she went to bed?
Andrea was awake for fourteen and one-half hours.

© Carson-Dellosa CD-3760   92

Answer Key

Name _____   Skill: Word Problems

Read the paragraph carefully, then answer the questions. Write **NG** (not given) if there is not enough information to answer the question.

Four children had a contest to see who could skate the most laps around the rink. Mr. Nerey kept the count for each child. These were the results: Charles skated 43 laps in one hour. Pam skated 16 laps and quit after 30 minutes. Jeremy skated for two hours and finished 67 laps. LeAnn skated for one and a half hours and made 86 laps.

1. **Which child skated the most laps?**
   LeAnn skated the most laps.

2. **Who skated for the longest time?**
   Jeremy skated for the longest time.

3. **How many laps did Charles and Jeremy skate altogether?**
   They skated one hundred ten laps altogether.

4. **How many laps did LeAnn and Pam skate altogether?**
   They skated one hundred two laps altogether.

5. **How many hours did all four children skate in all?**
   They skated five hours in all.

6. **How many laps did all four children skate in all?**
   They skated two hundred twelve laps in all.

7. **Who counted the number of laps for each child?**
   Mr. Nerey counted the number of laps.

8. **How many more laps did LeAnn skate than Charles?**
   LeAnn skated forty-three more laps than Charles.

© Carson-Dellosa CD-3760   93

Name _____   Skill: Word Problems

Read the paragraph and chart carefully, then answer the questions. Write **NG** (not given) if there is not enough information to answer the question.

Pat's friends held a frog jumping contest. Six frogs were entered. The results of the contest are listed on the chart at the right.

Spot	8 ft 3 in
Kicker	6 ft 8 in
Potsy	5 ft 2 in
Flaps	6 ft 6 in
Croaker	8 ft 4 in
Harvey	7 ft 9 in

1. **Which frog jumped the farthest?**
   Croaker jumped the farthest.

2. **Which frog had the shortest jump?**
   Potsy had the shortest jump.

3. **What is the name of the frog that came in second place?**
   Spot finished in second place.

4. **At what time was the jumping contest held?**
   NG

5. **How much farther did Harvey jump than Potsy?**
   He jumped two feet, seven inches farther.

6. **Which frogs jumped farther than 7 feet 2 inches?**
   Spot, Croaker, and Harvey jumped farther.

7. **How far did Flaps jump?**
   Flaps jumped six feet, six inches.

8. **In which town was the frog jumping contest held?**
   NG

© Carson-Dellosa CD-3760   94

Name _____   Skill: Word Problems

Read the paragraph carefully, then answer the questions. Write **NG** (not given) if there is not enough information to answer the question.

Mrs. White's third grade class held a bake sale this week. On Monday they sold 212 cupcakes. On Tuesday they sold 148 cupcakes. Wednesday was a slow day with only 43 cupcakes sold. The class did not sell cupcakes on Thursday. On Friday the group sold 271 cupcakes! They made a lot of money with cupcake sales.

1. **On which day did the class not sell cupcakes?**
   They did not sell cupcakes on Thursday.

2. **How many cupcakes did the class sell this week?**
   They sold six hundred seventy-four this week.

3. **On which day did they sell the most cupcakes?**
   They sold the most on Friday.

4. **How many cupcakes were sold on Tuesday and Wednesday together?**
   They sold one hundred ninety-one altogether.

5. **How many more cupcakes were sold on Friday than Monday?**
   They sold fifty-nine more on Friday.

6. **On which day did they sell the least cupcakes (not including Thursday)?**
   They sold the least on Wednesday.

7. **How many students are in Mrs. White's third grade class?**
   NG

8. **How many more cupcakes were sold on Monday than on Wednesday?**
   They sold one hundred sixty-nine more.

© Carson-Dellosa CD-3760   95

Name _____   Skill: Word Problems

Read the paragraph carefully, then answer the questions. Write **NG** (not given) if there is not enough information to answer the question.

Dotty made a quilt. She cut lots of material into small squares and sewed them together. All of the squares were the same size. The quilt had 143 blue squares, 22 yellow squares, 119 green squares, 38 orange squares, and 74 brown squares. It took Dotty 3 months to sew all the squares together! She keeps the quilt on her bed.

1. **How long did it take Dotty to sew the quilt squares?**
   It took her three months.

2. **How many of the squares were green?**
   One hundred nineteen squares were green.

3. **Which color did Dotty use the least?**
   She used yellow the least.

4. **Together, how many blue and orange squares are in the quilt?**
   One hundred eighty-one were blue and orange.

5. **How much did it cost to make the quilt?**
   NG

6. **How many squares did Dotty use in all?**
   She used three hundred ninety-six squares in all.

7. **How many more blue squares were used than brown squares?**
   Sixty-nine more blue squares were used.

8. **What was the size of each square?**
   They were all the same size.

© Carson-Dellosa CD-3760   96

Answer Key

Name _____   Skill: Word Problems

Read the paragraph carefully, then answer the questions. Write **NG** (not given) if there is not enough information to answer the question.

Sharon opened a lemonade stand in front of her house last summer. Sharon sold the lemonade for $1.00 per glass. Most of her customers were neighbors or family members. She made $15 in June, $22 in July, and $29 in August. Sharon used the money she made to buy a new bicycle!

1. **What kind of business did Sharon have last summer?**
   She had a lemonade stand.

2. **During which three months did Sharon sell lemonade?**
   She sold during June, July, and August.

3. **How much did Sharon charge for a glass of lemonade?**
   She charged one dollar per glass.

4. **What did Sharon do with the money she made selling lemonade?**
   She bought a new bicycle.

5. **During which month did Sharon make the most money?**
   She made the most during August.

6. **How much money did Sharon make for the month of June?**
   She made fifteen dollars.

7. **How many of the neighbors bought lemonade from Sharon?**
   NG

8. **How much money did Sharon make selling lemonade last summer?**
   She made sixty-six dollars in all.

© Carson-Dellosa CD-3760   97

$$\begin{array}{r} 2 \\ +\ 9 \\ \hline \end{array}$$

$$\begin{array}{r} 3 \\ +\ 3 \\ \hline \end{array}$$

$$\begin{array}{r} 3 \\ +\ 4 \\ \hline \end{array}$$

$$\begin{array}{r} 3 \\ +\ 5 \\ \hline \end{array}$$

$$\begin{array}{r} 3 \\ +\ 6 \\ \hline \end{array}$$

$$\begin{array}{r} 3 \\ +\ 7 \\ \hline \end{array}$$

$$\begin{array}{r} 3 \\ +\ 8 \\ \hline \end{array}$$

$$\begin{array}{r} 3 \\ +\ 9 \\ \hline \end{array}$$

$$\begin{array}{r} 4 \\ +\ 4 \\ \hline \end{array}$$

$$\begin{array}{r} 4 \\ +\ 5 \\ \hline \end{array}$$

$$\begin{array}{r} 4 \\ +\ 6 \\ \hline \end{array}$$

$$\begin{array}{r} 4 \\ +\ 7 \\ \hline \end{array}$$

$$\begin{array}{r} 4 \\ +\ 8 \\ \hline \end{array}$$

$$\begin{array}{r} 4 \\ +\ 9 \\ \hline \end{array}$$

$$\begin{array}{r} 5 \\ +\ 5 \\ \hline \end{array}$$

$$\begin{array}{r} 5 \\ +\ 6 \\ \hline \end{array}$$

8	7	6	11
12	11	10	9
11	10	9	8
11	10	13	12

3 − 1	3 − 2	3 − 3	4 − 1
© CD-3760	© CD-3760	© CD-3760	© CD-3760
4 − 2	4 − 3	4 − 4	5 − 1
© CD-3760	© CD-3760	© CD-3760	© CD-3760
5 − 2	5 − 3	5 − 4	5 − 5
© CD-3760	© CD-3760	© CD-3760	© CD-3760
6 − 1	6 − 2	6 − 3	6 − 4
© CD-3760	© CD-3760	© CD-3760	© CD-3760

3	0	1	2
© CD-3760	© CD-3760	© CD-3760	© CD-3760
4	0	1	2
© CD-3760	© CD-3760	© CD-3760	© CD-3760
0	1	2	3
© CD-3760	© CD-3760	© CD-3760	© CD-3760
2	3	4	5
© CD-3760	© CD-3760	© CD-3760	© CD-3760

$\begin{array}{r} 1 \\ \times\ 5 \\ \hline \end{array}$	$\begin{array}{r} 2 \\ \times\ 3 \\ \hline \end{array}$	$\begin{array}{r} 4 \\ \times\ 0 \\ \hline \end{array}$	$\begin{array}{r} 9 \\ \times\ 3 \\ \hline \end{array}$
© CD-3760	© CD-3760	© CD-3760	© CD-3760
$\begin{array}{r} 3 \\ \times\ 6 \\ \hline \end{array}$	$\begin{array}{r} 4 \\ \times\ 5 \\ \hline \end{array}$	$\begin{array}{r} 9 \\ \times\ 6 \\ \hline \end{array}$	$\begin{array}{r} 8 \\ \times\ 5 \\ \hline \end{array}$
© CD-3760	© CD-3760	© CD-3760	© CD-3760
$\begin{array}{r} 7 \\ \times\ 8 \\ \hline \end{array}$	$\begin{array}{r} 9 \\ \times\ 1 \\ \hline \end{array}$	$\begin{array}{r} 0 \\ \times\ 0 \\ \hline \end{array}$	−
© CD-3760	© CD-3760	© CD-3760	© CD-3760
+	>	<	=
© CD-3760	© CD-3760	© CD-3760	© CD-3760

27	0	6	5

40	54	20	18

minus	0	9	56

equals	less than	greater than	plus

adult	adjective	actual	ache
© CD-3760	© CD-3760	© CD-3760	© CD-3760
aunt	anxious	antonym	ant
© CD-3760	© CD-3760	© CD-3760	© CD-3760
beyond	beach	awful	author
© CD-3760	© CD-3760	© CD-3760	© CD-3760
break	brake	bowl	bottle
© CD-3760	© CD-3760	© CD-3760	© CD-3760

difficult	dine	distant	drum
© CD-3760	© CD-3760	© CD-3760	© CD-3760

duck	engine	entire	expense
© CD-3760	© CD-3760	© CD-3760	© CD-3760

feather	final	flour	flower
© CD-3760	© CD-3760	© CD-3760	© CD-3760

flute	forest	fragment	fuzz
© CD-3760	© CD-3760	© CD-3760	© CD-3760

subject	sway	swing	synonym
tasty	teeth	timid	tree
unusual	vanish	verb	victory
visitor	vowel	watch	whole

© CD-3760